In *From Mothers to Daughters,* Christina Ballinotti eloquently puts forth her concerns about family values in our current society. She advocates for a more mindful approach to motherhood and family life. She correctly identifies that we are undergoing a tremendous shift in society as consequential as the Copernican revolution when the earth was no longer viewed to be the center of the universe.

The globalization of the world and the shift in women's roles as they become more equal in the workforce has altered the traditional male and female responsibilities. The structure and functions of families is changing at an unprecedented rate. Some changes have been profoundly beneficial, while others have led to more isolation, unhappiness, and dysfunction in our core support system: the family.

From Mothers to Daughters urges women to understand the importance of their role as a mother and the impact they will have on their child's psychological development. Parenting is a privilege and should be entered into with maturity, commitment, and an education. Ms. Ballinotti provides a well-researched look into the role of the mother, grandmother, and father in raising a healthy child. She provides readers with an understanding of child and adolescent development, and she argues for the primary role of the mother.

As more and more women are combining motherhood and employment outside the house, we as a society need to be cognizant of the effects of our choices. As a physician and mother of two, I have struggled with how to balance these roles, and I laud Ms. Ballinotti for urging us all to continue the dialogue and focus on the healthy psychological development of our children.

Eva Ritvo, MD, Psychiatrist
Best-selling co-author of *The Beauty Prescription.*

From Mothers to Daughters

Christina Balinotti is an Argentine author and lecturer. She holds a bachelor's degree in social sciences with postgraduate studies in Psychology including 3 years at the Faculty of Philosophy and Literature in her native city of Buenos Aires. She also has ample knowledge in the field of quantum physics.

She has resided in Miami since the year 2000, where she works as an international analyst on Spanish-language TV and Radio, investigating the crimes and suicides of our young people and their relationship to maternal absence during a child's early years in this and in other developed societies.

Through her Foundation, *Feminidad Holística* (*Holistic Femininity*), Christina Balinotti organizes conferences and annual workshops at several Florida universities (FIU, UM, SUAGM) as well as in important venues in Miami for the purpose of educating women in the essential recovery of family values and in the pathways of holistic femininity, all free of charge.

In 2013 she hosted a radio show at *Radio Nova Internacional* as well as a weekly TV Show at Telemiami in which she, together with other professionals, including sociologists, historians and psychologists, analyzed the role of women in Western cultures. Proud mother and grandmother.

Holistic Femininity, presents:

FROM MOTHERS TO DAUGHTERS

The ABCs of Motherhood and Family Values

CHRISTINA BALINOTTI

Translated from the Spanish by Gilbert Grasselly

Holistic Femininity: A call to the family, headed by the mother. May she become the heart of world peace.

Translator's note: As the reader may be aware, in the Spanish language every word has gender. Even the word for child is either masculine or feminine (niño, niña). However, in Spanish the word niño can refer to any child. Therefore in the following translation, I have followed the lead of Spanish and have often used the pronoun "he" to refer to an individual baby or child. This is to minimize the possibly tiresome overuse of the combinations "he/she" "him/her," etc. I simply want the reader to know that as a translator I have no intention of emphasizing the male gender over the female, so every "he" can also be read as "she".

PUBLISHING HOUSE:
Alexandria Library (www.alexlib.com)

PHOTOGRAPHY:
Chaviano studio & production Corp.

ARTWORK by Elizabeth Menda
Signs Now

To mothers of the future. To the grandmothers and young daughters of today. To my dearly-loved Barbara and Petra, in the certainty that these lines will shine a beacon of hope on the pathways of their lives. Today and always.

Show me your mother's face
and I'll tell you who you are.
Kahlil Gibran

CONTENTS

FOREWORD

If we want a profession, we enroll in a university. You know that. Wishing is not enough. We must be trained. Get a degree. But, for the most important work of our lives—being parents—there are no schools or universities. As they say in my country, *"Estamos a la buena de Dios en el asunto"*—in other words, God help us. While a doctor studies many long years before attending to his first patient or a lawyer memorizes treaties and laws to help implement justice, we have children as if having them were enough. In this regard, culture is no help. Culture promotes economic development, success and competition for jobs. It provides courses and seminars to help us learn to be better negotiators, to earn big money. There is plenty of that and, let's be honest, money is necessary, but we must balance things. We must prioritize.

The Spanish philosopher Ortega y Gasset once said that to understand a problem it needs to be talked about. Therefore, we must talk about these issues so that we can understand each other as individuals and as a society. We must talk about the ignorance we suffer from in terms of parenting. We must talk about the social indifference to the absence of mothers and fathers in the home. We must talk about problems that batter us with their daily consequences: children and adolescents who run away, commit suicide, kill people or take drugs; about children who are beaten and abused, not only by sick family members outside the immediate family but also by the parents themselves. On the other hand, physical punishment as a disciplinary measure follows the known agenda. "A beating or a kiss can fix anything" goes one saying. But beatings, slapping and spankings are nothing more than momentary adult outbursts—an emotional loss of control by unguided parents who do what they can, based on what was done to them. With such actions, they fix nothing and do considerable damage. Beating is an indication of frustration. It reveals a lack of words to make oneself understood. Parents have not learned how to gain their children's trust, how to empathize with them in order to understand their issues. For this, parents need to spend time with them as well as physical and emotional availability.

"Out of sight, out of mind," the denial of these situations is a defense mechanism that keeps us from looking squarely at ourselves while we blame others for things that we, as parents, have failed to acknowledge within ourselves.

Too often, television and radio media reflect this painful reality but they accomplish nothing and change nothing. Our society is in a rush, making breakneck scientific and technological advances while families are caught in an equally precipitous decline of values, principles, self-criticism and a lack of appreciation of otherness. What is to become of all of us in the future? Will we become a community of beings with no emotional anchors, without roots, without feelings of belonging, without affection? Perhaps we are already suffering such a future. Do we want *to be* or do we want *to have*? This is the well-known dilemma posed by Jean Paul Sartre. The scientist Nikola Tesla expressed the hope that progress would mean contributing to improving the human condition, but he did not trust technology to contribute to this end. Although oftentimes technological advances give us excellent work tools, at other times they lead to a serious weakening of family relationships. Today our youth seek refuge in social networks, over-indulgence in their cravings for communication and dialogue. Parents, unlike modern-day gadgets, are almost never available. In principle, technology is supposed to improve the quality of our lives, but today it has become a nightmare for the family. It has become something dangerous because it hampers the development of those feelings that unite us in peaceful coexistence, with empathy, gratitude and compassion, based on healthy self-esteem. On the other hand, so-called online anonymity contributes to the aggravation of negative tendencies and dormant misguided inclinations. Today we know that children with severe psychiatric syndromes or certain kinds of personality disorders have a greater propensity of becoming violent if family circumstances incite it. On the other hand, they will become happy beings if they have caring parents who seek to help them and know how to limit them. Take the example of the Sandy Hook tragedy in which an autistic youth kills his mother and his classmates then commits suicide. We know that 20-year-old Adam Lanza lived as a recluse in the basement of his home where he spent time watching violent video games. This is the worst kind of activity for someone who suffers from such a condition, which, because of its clinical characteristics, led him to seek isolation and confinement. World leaders sent their condolences to the people of this town. Pope Benedict XVI begged God to bring comfort, and President Obama declared that something must be done. Gun control was the main issue. No one came forth to articulate thoughts about parental education. No governmental organization seems to be qualified to teach us how to educate healthy children, as well as those suffering from psychological disorders and psychiatric illnesses. Blaming ones children is not the solution. On the contrary, we must rethink our responsibilities in these matters. Many such killings could be prevented! We need to accept the truth of the following statement: Three essential figures are associated with the life of a child—the *mother*, the *father* and the *teacher*. However, note that the teacher, no matter how important he or she is, is not the first educator. This task falls to the parents, starting with the most significant figure in a child's life—the mother. Today, most mothers are not at home during the first few years of their children's life. When I talk about "mothers at home" I am not referring to the homebound wife slaves of the 1960's. I am talking about a healthy middle ground; for example, a mother being with her children most of the time during their early childhood as a facilitator, and being there for his or her "slow liftoff" as each stage separates in the ascent of the child, rising slowly. Everything in life involves processes. Today we live too fast, under too much pressure, always watching the clock. Life for most has become a series of obligations and duties, forcing us to live lives that are increasingly more hurried. In all spheres of life, we have become accustomed to demanding rapid solutions because we don't have time to wait. Urgency and stress rule our lives. It is sad and disturbing that this haste applies mainly to the lives of women. Because of this situation, we women still have not found our inner balance to know who we are, what we want and what our substantial role is in society. We are like a delicate musical instrument that no one knows how fine tune. You, my female friend, have never been able to produce your best notes or melodies in the shared symphony of personal and family life. And that is what this this book is all about—to enable you to hear the ringing of a different kind of bell; to catch sight of that beacon shining in the darkness; to help you create better relationships with your children and to enrich your role as a mother when you feel confused and don't know which way to turn. However, perhaps everything has gone well for you and you are the exception to the rule; still something in this book may come as a pleasant surprise and be something that can help you. It is hoped that the female legacy of From Mothers to Daughters will be a testament to peace, an affirmation of life and of family unity.

As a culture, we have given up on the idea of moving forward together, sacrificing this concept for the sake of individualism. We have not acknowledged that the plan of the universe is holistic—one of working and progressing together, where everyone has his or her place and an assigned task to carry out. The family, as such, should be a reflection of universal equilibrium, of the very creation—*night-day, sun-moon, female-male*—each with its different role and function.

In our current individualistic social environment and, again, lacking education in parenting, many independent women, living under optimal economic conditions, yet with very little available time, think about having children in the absence of a father. In some cases, these can be test tube babies engendered either anonymously or by a known donor, such as a friend or a former husband. Such children are the children of desire—personal desire—which, although valid, cannot coexist with the idea of committed motherhood. Even in a sound marriage, any biological or adopted children should be conceived or raised responsibly, subordinating desire to conscientious family planning. What do I mean by this? Say you are a single woman and your economic success is the result of long work hours outside the home. What, in such a case, would be the object of bringing a child into the world and letting a nanny or your mother raise it? The most meaningful duty of our lives—mothering—should not be handled in the same way we buy a house or a car. It does not mean the pleasure of becoming a parent as one who has the pleasure of acquiring a new purse. A well-known Argentine psychologist, Pablo Cazau wrote, with a touch of irony that, after the gifts of a nightstand and the traditional silver cutlery, a baby is the first "gift" newlyweds receive that cannot be gotten rid of so easily.

In light of the circumstances described above, a question arises: Who dares to think differently? Within ourselves, we carry some powerful *software* that is very difficult to extract. *Mea culpa.* I, too, have experienced these things, although under different circumstances. I also raised my first son on sheer intuition, struggling with my own youthfulness and desire to achieve. I was 21 years of age and was acquainted with hundreds of theories regarding early childhood education, but I was lacking in experience and no specific professional written guidelines were available to me. I thought that the mere act of having a baby would help me overcome my own insecurities and that I would be able to bring him up. Then I fully realized that I was the one who must solve his problems and must help him meet his basic needs without reservations, even though suffering from sleeplessness and exhaustion, but I was there at his side and taking charge. Above all, I knew I must forget myself, that my wish to be happy did not apply. Even my personal self-fulfillment did not depend on his company or his presence in this world. I finally understood that love is not enough. Love has its own contradictory rules, its own kind of rebellion. It has a way of pulling us back into our own EGO and drawing our attention away from the needs of others. It is definitely essential, but it is not enough. In the name of love, countless atrocities are committed every day. So it was, at that time, that I imagined creating a *University for the Family* that offers a required degree course that must be taken before one can marry. It would be given by professionals in an academic environment with specialized courses lasting no fewer than 24 months. Over the years, and because of family obligations, the idea was put on hold but it was always there, latent. Now that my children are grown and family structures everywhere continue to deteriorate, it's time for me to get down to work. It's time to lay the foundations for an academic program designed to assist in understanding the emotions and behaviors of raising infants and children, and your own emotions—mother of the future—to get to know your own self, to know, at the outset, whether or not you are prepared for motherhood. To learn how to handle anxiety in the face of your child's demands and, essentially, to know who he is and what he needs at every stage of his development. That is what this this book is all about—planting seeds, building a foundation and inviting everyone to work together in carrying out this ambitious project. Again, just as we must train for a profession we should also receive training in parenting and, to my female readers, I especially emphasize, training in *how to be a mother.* This undertaking and responsibility has been cheapened in our society and has been handed over to strangers. We women of today go to work early in the morning and leave our kids in the care of nannies who leave their own kids with other women, and so on, in a hellish sequence. We resort to daycare and juggle things because the money is not enough. As our children mature, their frustrations increase. There are gaps and shortcomings, all of which lead to adolescent violence and to our constant feelings of guilt as mothers.

Therefore, we need to bring about fundamental changes in our cultural thinking, a paradigm shift in order to rethink how we have lived our lives thus far. We need to redefine the meaning of the word *mother.* We need to start over. As the saying goes, "back to basics." We are living in a time of great civilizational transformations. The time has come. We must not allow the breakneck pace of modern progress to leave families exposed to these raging storms.

The situation, as I see it is, in a way, comparable to the Copernican revolution that took place during the Renaissance when the geocentric theory was replaced by the heliocentric one presented by Copernicus. At that moment in history, Earth ceased to be the center of the planetary system. The sun now occupied that position. The concept was so revolutionary that even today, when we talk about drastic 360-degree changes we refer to them as Copernican changes. Accordingly, the very meaning of the word "planet" was redefined. From being a wandering star, as its etymology suggests, it became a star orbiting the sun. In our own time, the hoped-for revolution must be one of values and ideals, one of a loving, feminine moral philosophy. A Copernican transformation must take place that rethinks the position of our children in the social cosmos, from that of wandering stars lost in cyberspace to stars circling in orderly fashion around the axis of the family. The expectation must be to heal a world lacking any charitable cultural heritage to transmit, and without heirs wanting to receive it. Nothing is permanent. Everyone lives his or her own life as they wish; it doesn't matter who they hurt along the way. Consider what I have said about this: "The illiterates of the future won't be those who are unable to read or write but those who don't know how to contribute or cooperate." We seek personal accomplishment in a culture of competitiveness. However, through *cooperation* we live shared lives by teaching others how to be of assistance, how to cooperate, how to be truly sociable: *Please. May I? Sorry. Thank you.* Moreover, who better than we women to impart these time-honored lessons of love and wisdom, of patience and compassion, of teaching children, husbands and friends? Women and mothers—we are the teachers of the ABCs of family life and values. It is a cultural imperative that we prepare ourselves for our maternal role. I would almost dare to say that we have a shared interest and that the survival of the species depends on this.

Before continuing, let us quickly consider the historic moment that we now share—the era of globalization. It is a moment of transition referred to by some sociologists as *postmodern*, which began in 1989 with the ending of the Cold War, the ultimate expression of which was the fall of the Berlin Wall.

Unlike the past, the world is moving towards unity and evident interdependence among the countries that encircle the globe. This growing planetary movement toward unity manifests itself in economic, technological, political and cultural interconnectivity. Thanks to the Internet and the social media revolution, news of what happens in a remote village in China is available immediately everywhere else on the planet.

It is paradoxical and perplexing that such a network of global integration and the multinational corporations and consumer societies it serves, has not yet succeeded in globalizing specific values and principles, the great philosophies of life that promote human relationships beyond commercial trade, that help our fellow citizens, that help us raise our children, that help us care for the environment. If indeed something has gone global, in this regard, it is urban violence and individual isolation. We find ourselves alone in an efficiently connected world in which we are, nevertheless, hopelessly isolated. In the words of Argentine philosopher Santiago Kovadoff, "We live in a world of silence filled with the din of words"—loud noises communicating nothing, a din that stuns us and drenches us in indifference and anomie. We have chosen to sever human ties and, in their place, attach gadgets and phones to our ears to avoid sharing or hearing so that we can be alone, and not be just "me and my circumstances" in the words of Ortega y Gasset, but *just me*—to be insular and withdrawn, a slave to my phone and my Facebook. In this regard, author Alvin Toffler in his book "Future Shock" predicted a world of social and individual trauma.

The Berlin Wall came crashing down. A few other walls also tumbled. Others still exist waiting to be brought down. However, the only impregnable and accepted walls remaining are those that we human beings have built and continue to erect among ourselves.

Disillusioned with religion and politics we seek refuge in material possessions, in being consumers; in sex disconnected from love. Without faith, without God and without exemplary leaders, we reject spirituality, morality and parenthood. Authority in the home has become obsolete. Children dictate their own rules and we, the parents, abide by them. We confuse freedom of expression with freedom to do whatever we feel like doing. Divorced parents feel guilty and think that the best way to patch things up is to do nothing, God forbid that our children be offended and ask the judge to give them a different set of parents.

This is the world in which families evolve, or just the opposite, regress, into cultural milieus previously inhabited, or perhaps never experienced. This is where my proposal comes in—at this inescapable point where *what we are* meets up with *what we should be*. I invite you to join me.

THE CRUCIAL ROLE OF THE MOTHER AND THE IMPORTANCE OF THE FATHER

Why should I get married?

A life of emotional health for your future child begins as a conscious family project. Of course you can marry for reasons foreign to the idea of family, such as sharing in projects and outings, having a live-in companion, or to avoid living alone. In any case, it is only you, the woman who will either benefit or be hurt. But things are different when a child is involved. When this is the case, your partner must be chosen for his human qualities such as being supportive and having high moral principles.

You must be able to guarantee to your child that his father or your male partner is a man of values, who contributes to creating an ideal climate for your child's emotional development. So, be rational. Don't look for the father of your future children in some *playboy* who loves nightlife and easy women. On the other hand, if you sincerely want to be a mother, you must plan ahead to create a favorable economic situation. You must be able to have your child by your side during its early years and not leave him and go rushing off to work soon after he is born. It follows that if your economic resources are limited, you and your partner must try to make sure that they are adequate before you marry him and have that baby. "Where two can eat, three can" is not an applicable aphorism when it comes time to bringing a child into the world. In the following section, you will see why this is true.

Is there such thing as maternal instinct?

Maternal instinct, as such, does not exist. It can only develop in the context of a stimulating and loving home environment where a mother gives priority to her children. It is not something innate that we carry within. We either learn about mothering or miss this lesson in our own families, particularly in the relationships generated among mother, daughter and grandmother. When it is not learned, it explains why so many women abandon their offspring and, in some extreme cases, even kill them. Women such as these did not have a mother who loved and respected them nor did they have a mother model to inspire them. Quite the contrary, they must have had an unfeeling and negligent mother. Even as late as the seventeenth century, mothers could kill their offspring without blame or punishment. The Greek tale "Medea and Jason" is a well-known one in which Medea kills her children to avenge Jason. The lack of a motherly instinct provides us with a greater understanding of adoptive mothers who are affectionately maternal with their children—mothers who most certainly, in their own homes, acquired this crucial inclination to care for their offspring.

So, you see, "maternal instinct" is a cultural construct, the purpose of which is to help mothers ensure their family's stability and emotional health. What definitely does exist in human beings is the strong biological urge to *reproduce* which assures the continuation of the species. Such an urge, as it applies to women, makes most of them want to bear children, regardless of the consequences. In Spanish there is a saying that a newborn always arrives holding a loaf of bread—wrongly trusting in the child's destiny merely due to the good fortune of its having been born.

If we assume that maternal instinct is learned and not biological, then once we have had a child, its future education and learning will depend, dear friend and mom, on the lessons that you yourself learned from your own mother. So, in most cases, discounting the presence of any kind of psychiatric disorder, maternal behavior in today's societies generally reveals two kinds of mother-child relationships: the unattended child who is forced to grow up too soon and the spoiled one who never grows up.

As with every life experience, motherhood must also be a matter of balance. Leaving small children in the daily care of strangers is not a good idea, but neither is it a good idea to keep them forever at your side, thus preventing them from being able to grow and mature independently. Going to extremes is a typical mistake of human societies, such as in cases where children are forced to grow up too soon—which is the majority—and the pampered ones whose dreams and goals have to be put on hold to make up for the shortcomings of the mother. Later, such children, as adults, try to prolong the indulgences and comforts of their infancy. Let's take look at the first category.

The unattended child, forced to grow up too soon

With the rising divorce rate, with an increase in single-parent households and female economic liberation, a new type of orientation for motherhood has come to the fore. The way things are, children enjoy a good material standard of living but lose quality filial relationships, especially the daughters who are taught to be good providers but not how to be good mothers. They are taught to grow up fast because there is no mom at home. If we don't take action now, these young girls, when they reach adulthood, will impart the same lifestyle to their own children who, in turn, will be taught mostly how to compete and make lots of money. They will be taught to value material welfare over family and over the love of children. The daughters will learn to reject and cover up their female cycles because they interfere with the demanding rules of the workplace. At the other end of the social scale we find those moms with little income who are left with no other option but to leave their little ones in the care of strangers or relatives so they can hold down jobs.

Some time ago, while participating in a television show, I heard the sad story of a 9-year old boy who used to come home from school around midday with his little brother in tow. Invariably, before heading home to their apartment dwelling he would stop by the fast food place on the corner, and there he would buy two hamburgers and French fries. Too many children come home from school to an empty house! How many more such children get their meals and snacks from an indifferent babysitter with her own bundle of worries who imparts to the children her own beliefs and priorities according to her own lifestyle and customs, which are nearly always different from those of the children's mother. Here I exclude the cases of child abuse which have been detected by some parents who have the means wherewith to install cameras allowing them to have some degree of control over their nannies.

For both boys and girls, the absence of parents—especially that of the mother during their formative years—has become a public health concern affecting our entire society. This topic is like hot bread that we pass around quickly but is not brought up in our political, economic or social discourse. If it is talked about, it is just to place the blame for problems on children and adolescents. "I work, I burn myself out and you,

you behave badly, you don't study; all you do is look for trouble." We need to think about these things. The children are not at fault, nor are you, teammate Mom. Things are this way because of the demands of creating and maintaining material well-being. It is like the immense pressure of a torrential river that surges over us and overwhelms us. But in spite of this, if you are determined enough, you can slow down this torrent and make changes that will benefit your children.

The solution is so simple and so obvious that it may seem incredible. Just consider. This is what it's all about: We must choose; it's either *prevention* or a *palliative*. Prevention means to avoid having a child if, for economic reasons, you are unable fulfill your primary maternal duties or you have some other binding commitment that prevents you from doing so. Palliatives refer to things that you *can* do—that is, taking actions to compensate for your absence from the home. I will leave you with some tips here which I will explain in detail further on.

You must be willing to sacrifice your personal freedom so that you can be with your children, especially the youngest ones. If you can't share lunch or dinner with them, then sit next to them at the family table when you get home. Share some refreshments, some ice cream, cookies or fruit juice with your little boy or girl. Share something pleasant with them that you have experienced during the day. If you think that, because they are small, they might not understand, it doesn't matter. They will, at least, feel your energy and your desire to communicate with them, and they will appreciate it. If your children are sick, don't report to work. Talk to the children's teachers about how they are doing. Assert yourself as an involved mother who is active in school affairs. Don't be afraid of getting up from a business meeting in order to attend a school party or pick up the kids at school. We must get employers and corporations used to respecting the mother's role, rather than allowing them to undermine it. I'm sure you feel overwhelmed by the demands of your productive job and by your financial responsibilities, or perhaps you feel the giddiness of a successful career that you don't feel like giving up because it gives you a feeling of satisfaction. That's fine, but, in the end, the interests of the child must prevail. You brought that baby into this world and that is something you cannot neglect. Allow your child to maintain the proper pace of his tender years. There should be no haste, no rush, because, later on, such haste can cost you dearly. Think more clearly about having another baby. Wait. No matter how much money you earn or how many high-class nannies you can afford, don't have that baby if you think it will be difficult for you to have him at your side during his first six years of his life. Societies are made up of adults who were once children. We must think deeply about these matters.

The spoiled child who never grows up

En In this second category we find mothers who are dissatisfied with their personal life—unproductive women who almost invariably feel a lack of true love and who cling to their children as their only source of fulfillment. They overprotect them and go far beyond what is normal or necessary. Their children become like a lifeline for them. In such situations, what are we teaching the child? We are teaching emotional dependency, emotional addiction. Because we women, my dear female friend, feel unfulfilled. We yearn for recognition, for social visibility and for sympathy from someone who will love us and inspire us to flourish. Who can say you are to blame if you find yourself in a situation like this! No matter, for the good of your family, in the lines that follow there is some useful information that may help you to modify to some degree any similar situation you may be facing.

We could cite many examples, including an array of children's competitions, now very much in vogue on U.S. television. They resemble the so-called reality shows that reveal the maneuvers that moms go through for the unwitting purpose of achieving success through their children. Here's the first thing you should know: A young child does not have the maturity to choose a career. You, dear friend and mother, are free to choose what you want for yourself. As for your child, he or she needs your love and will do anything to please you.

If she is a girl she will tell everybody that she loves modeling or dancing, and will get involved in any activity you suggest. Let your child be a child! If you yourself have not been able to fulfill your own childhood dreams, don't force them onto your child! To do so is a form of abuse. Recapture that forgotten calling of yours, and dare to fulfill your dreams after the children are out of the house and you are in an "empty nest". If you're not sure just what your calling is, think about your past and your teenage accomplishments. You may find a sleeping interest there, a forgotten inclination. Remember, children cannot be photocopies of their parents; they must be originals of themselves.

So if you, dear mom, find yourself saying that your child is everything to you, then stop and seek help. Your children cannot be everything to you. If they are, you are burdening them with a charge they cannot possibly bear. Children forced to grow up while bearing the burden of making Mom happy are deprived of their responsibility to seek their own destiny and calling; if these are put on hold and in a limbo, they may never be fulfilled. Children in such situations are those who never marry, who never really think about their inmost desires. Whether consciously or unconsciously, they know that as long as they dutifully play the role assigned to them by their mother, their future will be good. There is no doubt that this is a very dangerous state of affairs. Furthermore, we run the risk of turning our children into narcissistic adolescents susceptible to severe behavioral problems.

Alfred Adler, a disciple of Freud's, said that overindulged teenagers are the most dangerous members of our communities because, since they are the main attraction in the family, they haven't learned how to cooperate—the sole purpose of their existence being to ensure the happiness of their mother and, by extension, their own personal fulfillment. Such youth put forth no effort on their own behalf and do not think about their future. They just hang around and carry on, never giving serious thought to what will become of themselves. It is a kind of melancholy that Baudelaire speaks of in his book "The Flowers of Evil" Weariness and boredom. Just killing time, not doing much of anything, putting forth little or no effort and having no worries. Such attitudes are typical of youthful immaturity, but they can become afflictive and devastate their lives as adults. In such situations, one might say that the umbilical cord was never cut; but there is an emotional attachment which is no less powerful.

The balancing act of modern mothers

We women are a living balancing act, no doubt about it. In both hands we balance different responsibilities—our personal fulfillment in one and our children in the other. We think that we can do it all, but we cannot. We must prioritize.

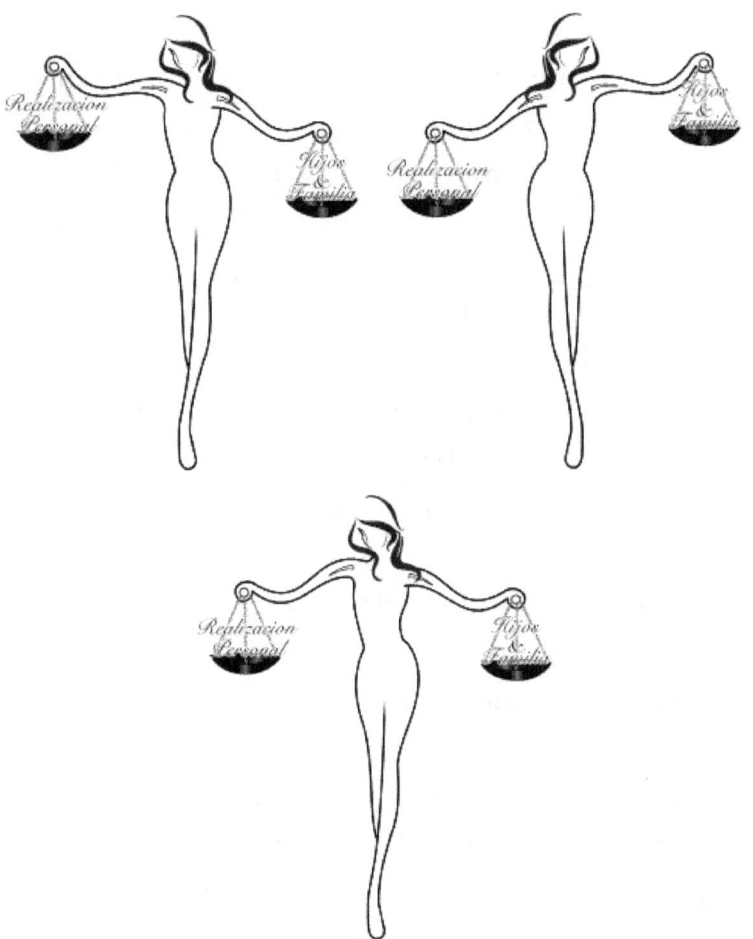

At certain times in your life you will create space for your calling, and when starting a new family, you will yield that space to your children. This is difficult to acknowledge because, as stated earlier, in today's world our efforts are constantly directed at our work with the above-mentioned consequences for our children. So, where to start? The first step is to walk away from stereotypes, such as the notorious examples of TV shows, movies and magazines, especially women in pants. Get to know yourself, who you are, where you are headed and what your purpose in life is; by doing this, you will begin to make healthy choices and will learn to be honest with yourself.

If you decide to become a mother, remember the guidance from the Bible. There is a time to sow and a time to reap. In the sowing season, take care of the seed, water it, guide the young shoot; then later in the season you can leave it in the confident knowledge that no wind will knock it down. This is the heartbeat of the Universe, the Holistic creation.

Mother - everyone's first love

You may wonder at my insistence on the person and role of the mother during the early years of a new human life. Its importance is momentous and yet is largely unacknowledged. In these pages you will find detailed psychological reasons and explanations for this assertion. I can tell you, for now, that the mother is the first love for both boys and girls—the first being on which the infant directs his energy, his attention, against whom he nestles. In the beginning, the infant explores the mother's body, getting to know the area between the arms that hold him and the little world around him. Later on he will push himself away from those arms and dare to begin trying to explore his surroundings. Mom is the model and fertile ground for the shaping of all the future relationships in his life. Unconsciously, we look for something of our own mother in the partners we end up choosing—something that resonates—a distant echo, a look, an aroma. Adult independence is achieved after having depended enough on our mothers during our early development. A healthy mother gradually transforms her child into an independent being—one who is unique and original. She, through physical and emotional stimuli, shapes and enables the development of her child's personality. If an individual did not have the good fortune of having a mother in charge of this transformative role, problems will arise later in life: depression; difficulty relating; an inability to experience pleasure. The individual will continue searching for his mother in the environments of his adult life, among his friends and girlfriends; in his elderly mother, who will be unable to provide him with such stimulus, or he will become a normal adult—having evolved from a child with a good mother—one who facilitated his leaving the nest—and will be able to leave home as a well-assured individual, able to create his own family, perhaps be able to live in another country and be happy there; but only if his mother has known how to be a constant presence for him, using patience and giving constant encouragement to his mind and heart; that is, has been able to establish an "optimal distance" so that her child can break away when the time comes. This is the ulti-mate destiny, the final liftoff for every human being.

Mothers are sponges

A second major factor in the psychological develop-ment of the child is that its mother must be an source of repose and peacefulness. Babies are born with wild, untidy instincts, squirming and prone to anxiety. They have no way of controlling aggressiveness, which, in-credibly, animal offspring do have. We mothers, there-fore, must absorb a newborn's aggressive impulses and lovingly redirect them. When he screeches, cries and thrashes about, he must be comforted. You assure him that everything is all right. You sing to him. You stroke him gently on the back. By doing these things you calm him down. If he bites you or hits you with his little hand, you say to him, "No, not like that." We moth-ers, like sponges, absorb the extraordinary impulses of our baby, including his aggressiveness in response to a perplexing world and toward his own small body that he has little control over. But if you, mother-friend, become irritated, scream or cry; if you become angry and your anxiety spills over, your child's own natural impulses will only intensify. Later on, when he is an adolescent, aggressiveness and belligerence will be his letter of introduction. We see manifestations of this violence in the teenagers around us. So, what is go-ing on? In today's world, women do not stay at home.

We women identify with the competitive life of men and their strengths. We follow them and try to imitate them. Men have done well in their expansionist role; they have done well as inventors and creators of civilized spaces and as inventors of technologies, and they have made many positive contributions to health and the workplace. This is impressive. Thank God for men! But…, my lady friends, we are different. We are fountains of life and know about the soul; we are inspirers of wholesome love and hope. We teach the world how to go from "I" to "We." We teach patience and the art of loving. We can achieve professional success either before or after bearing children. We can earn good money, imitate the men, be muscular and still be curvy. It's confusing but this is how it is. It's fashionable and feels good. We feel we must accept these things. But if we want to have the world's adventures at our feet, then we must put off having children, put this wish on hold. Everything you want in life will come along if you can abstain from the cultural imperative of multi-tasking. Just what is this? It's doing many things almost perfectly, all at the same time. Of course this is impossible, yet it is exactly what we try to do. Our functioning brain tells us "No!" but our culture demands it of us. It is forced upon us until, when, finally, we reach home, exhausted, fueled only by cortisol and adrenaline—and the children still haven't done their homework, then there is a meal to prepare…., this is how it goes. Now, calm down and read on. Charity, properly understood, begins at home. That's what my grandmother used to say. And the first home, the first setting for the formation of a family is what I call a "marital unit." What does this mean?

Introducing the concept of *marital unit*

Living together means accepting the presence of a new "other" in the home. That "other," in addition to the wife or husband individually can be termed a *marital unit*, which is a combination of the two. It consists of the interaction and interfacing of the strengths and weaknesses of both the husband and the wife. When faced with a problem, the couple as a *marital unit* will respond differently from the way each partner would respond individually. Both partners—husband and wife— must work unitedly to keep their family unit in balance. For them to be able do this implies a degree of personal surrender, selflessness, commitment and, above all, negotiation. This is especially true where children are concerned. A continuous re-negotiating of circumstances and personal desires must prevail throughout our lives, since our lifecycles, with their changes and transformations, mean that the father and mother must learn to agree on new goals and how to face life's changes, including death, menopause and children leaving home, moving to a different location which requires adaptability, flexibility and recognition of the value of change without neglecting basic traditions and ties that help us remain connected as a society. Today, we have replaced negotiation of goals, patience and conciliation with rapid divorce and fighting. Erich Fromm, in his book *The Art of Loving*, says that patience is an art we must develop in order to be able to love. After a few years, you may feel the need for a change in your life and in your routines; in short, you may have an unfulfilled dream. If problems arise, it is probably time for some healthy re-negotiating. Sit down together, have a cup of coffee and have a frank and honest dialogue with each other. Dialogue is a great friend of human relationships and is an unconditional ally of the family. Look, you tell him (or her), this is what I want (or need), and I'm asking for your support. Bear in mind that most human conflict arises out of a lack of communication. *To communicate* means to share and *take communion* together in the chalice that is life.

The importance of the father

Before proceeding, and having emphasized the quintessential role of the mother, we will now proceed to champion the *role of the father*—a role which in this society and others has all but been ignored, a society in which sexual differentiation has fallen into disuse.

Clearly, couples are complementary. Each partner has a role to play. *Sun-Moon. Night-Day.* The father lays down certain rules, and frames things. He is the runway from which his son or daughter taxis and takes off from the family up into the world. You, Mom, bestow love, show patience and are the engine of life for your child. You're also the hangar, the computer that reaches around the world. You, father-friend, facilitate the sacred and primary link that is created between your wife and your child during the first six years of his or her life. Thanks to you, your child will learn to respect and appreciate the prohibitions of human society. This is the *role of the father*—a function which has all but been forgotten in today's world. Certainly, persistent sexism has contributed to creating this state of affairs. The abuse of women is also commonplace. Perhaps these phenomena have led us to rejecting any degree of authority coming from the male sector. However, when a woman has given birth to a child she should step back and acknowledge the authority of the father-husband-partner in the home. Not authority over you, the mother, of course, but over your children. Society must have rules: traffic lanes to follow, complementary roles and tasks. In any case, differences are crucial. Consider this: The structure of a family can be viewed as a triangular formation. That is, mother-father-child each with his or her role to play and his or her own place in the family hierarchy. In this regard, Mom bestows tenderness and Dad enforces the rules. For the father to set down rules means that, while stepping aside so that his spouse can engross herself with rearing the little one during the first six years of life, he will undertake a series of maneuvers to help her gradually extract herself from her symbiosis with the child. In the case of a male child, the father will put in extra effort and will take him out to play ball, go to a baseball game, go fishing or biking, and he will make sure he no longer shares Mom's bed, if this is the case. By doing this he is letting the child know: Mom is my wife. One day when you grow up you will find your own partner outside the home. The taboo on incest is at the very foundation of every human society, with very few historical exceptions, such as that of ancient Egypt. It is a universal rule by which nature reigns supreme over itself, creating a more complex structure than the simple ones of the animal world. In the West, it is the father is who must enforce this hierarchy, even in cases where the son insists on seeking refuge in Mom's lap, even if it hurts Mom to push him away. Indeed, the son must marry outside the home in order to contribute to the advancement of the social dynamic. This is a fundamental law that the father enforces. Of course, in a jungle setting or in primitive communities, such rules may not apply. But, incest is definitely taboo in the great majority of cultures.

The female child who feels the need to identify with a mother figure, that is, to emulate it, can stay closer to and stay longer with her mother, go with her to the hairdresser or go shopping with her beyond the age of five or six. However, in due time, a cutoff point will have to be reached. And, of course, this implies a corresponding distance from the father as well. A wholesome dad must himself follow this rule with respect to his daughter. A small 5-year old girl told her father, "When I grow up I'm going to marry you because mommy will be too old." As you can see, the human family retains remnants of those primitive beings we once were which, no doubt, inhabit our collective unconsciousness. In some Latin American countries it is quite common for fathers to use the term "*novia*" [girlfriend or sweetheart] when referring to their daughters.

For both boys and girls their father's involvement in their lives is crucial. But the first love for both boys and girls is their mother. Therefore, because of the nature of the primary maternal bond, mothers who have developed a strong maternal instinct often regard their offspring as extensions of themselves. In some cases, this attitude continues beyond prudent and necessary age limits. When this happens, the father's obligation is to disconnect and undo these kinds of "attachments"—the fusion between a mother and her son or daughter. Unless rules are set down by the father, we cannot properly participate in the life and society or submit to the imperatives of language: "*I'm Johnny, the son, (the brother, the nephew)*," etc. "I have my place, my name and last name, in the family setting," just as a subject, verb and predicate have their place in a sentence so that when we express ourselves, we make sense. It is Dad who helps us detach ourselves from that close and necessary bond with Mom which otherwise might never come to an end. There can be no doubt that maternal love creates and nurtures, and that paternal rules enable us to express ourselves in society as individuals having our own desires, instead of merely being the objects of those of our mothers.

What about negligent mothers who abandon their young children? Children also depend on their father to the same degree to encourage the mother in creating that basic maternal bond, to inspire her to remain with her children during the first six years of their lives. Sometimes, the father might have to hold down more than one job so that his wife won't have to work long hours away from home. These are issues that must be discussed and communicated. Ideally, effective dialogue should be established prior to marriage and before children come along so that husband and wife can truly get to know each other.

The mother is a custodian. She is a port, a beach. But her son or daughter belongs to the seas, and just like a ship must eventually cut the riggings and set sail. If, by age thirty a son is still attached to the mother-nurse of his tender years, he will never be able to create his own roadmap or his own individual project. In order for a person to know who he or she is, an optimal distance must be reached from his or her first love—Mom. Similarly, a son or daughter can only achieve independence if they have had enough time with Mom. Such is the nature of life in society and in the natural world. Puppies leave their mother when the time comes to do so—neither before nor after. In this regard, we humans have altered our biology beyond belief. We aim for our children to be independent by age seven or eight or else we keep them at home until they are forty. Think of your child as a ship going from the shipyard out to the pier. One day you'll watch him sail off to distant ports, to his destination on some far-away shore. Your eyes will follow him, but don't try to stop his departure.

You ask, dear reader, how you can give life to this paternal role if you are a widow, a single mother, divorced or perhaps your spouse has a job that takes him away from home for extended periods of time. Well, with the first two options you can turn to your own father as a reference, or to a priest, a brother or a friend. Or maybe you know a committed couple who can help you fill the void. This effort depends, of course, on the quality of the individual and the relationship he or she is able to establish with your son or daughter. Similarly, if the father's work keeps him away from home, you can create this paternal function based on your speech, on the words you use. If it becomes necessary to scold your child, remind him, "What would Dad say if he saw you?" or "Daddy would not approve of such behavior." Believe me; words such as these are very effective because through them, you create the symbolic presence of the father.

Of course I am referring to mothers whose being alone has been imposed upon them by the circumstances of a challenging life. If you, lady-friend, have money, are single and successful and want to bear a child without having a father in the mix, or if you're thinking about adopting, ponder and think about what you have just read. A human being is much more than the product of the union of two genetic cells, much more than a joining of bodily fluids. To have a baby is a vital organic project resulting from the union of a man and a woman who are fully committed to each other and practicing responsible parenthood.

It has been said that children are a product of life. I believe that life receives them in its bosom after long years of parental care. Everything they achieve, therefore, will be the result of whatever training they receive at home. Don't sentence your child to having to feel different, trying to fill a void, an unnecessary gap left by Dad that will be there forever.

The "maternalized" father

Fatherhood has undergone serious rethinking in recent decades. This is due in particular to the greater economic independence of women. In many respects, the quality of bonding between fathers and their children has improved with increased dialogue and intimacy.

But the core of the issue—and I'm referring to the fatherly task of cutting the psychological umbilical cord between mother and baby and its consequences—remains to be seen. A "maternalized" father is one who has been distracted from playing his fundamental role, namely, helping his children to be on their way to deeper involvement in the social world in a mature and balanced way. In psychoanalytical terms, this is known as the "law of the father."

A son who doesn't abide by this law of the father may want to belong to the social order but misdirects himself by joining fanatical sects, gangs, lawbreakers or—as we have so sadly seen—fundamentalist terrorist groups. Someone must lay down the law for him. This is how we've been programmed. The mother cannot perform both fundamental roles—nor can the father. In the face of uncertainty we turn to the divine creation. Biology endowed woman with breasts with which to nourish and a matrix in which to create life. To man it gave strong arms and hormones making it possible for him to conquer, hunt and gather food. I am not opposed to female independence. I, too, am an independent woman. What I am opposed to is female independence at the expense of the children. Everything in its own good time. We must be cautious. A father raising a child can be a wonderful solution for a mother head of the household; but eventually we must ask ourselves whether such an arrangement is beneficial for the child.

We must ask ourselves whether having a father and a mother performing different roles according to their sex, may not be an invention of our culture but a psycho-biological necessity.

If a human couple found itself in the middle of a desert island each would immediately assume his or her natural role. For instance, he will build a safe shelter and go out hunting for food, and she will keep an orderly shelter and adorn her head with flowers. The great circle of life is a wheel of contrasts. This is the nature of our human essence which civilizations, as they unravel, feel they must reject or change.

CHAPTER II

WHAT A WOMAN NEEDS TO KNOW BEFORE BECOMING A MOTHER

Emotional DNA

It's everything you've ever experienced. Every joy and sorrow—traumas, frustrations or satisfactions—all of them are a kind of *emotional DNA* that you will pass on to your infant with every beat of your heart during your pregnancy and as you raise him or her. My female friend, if you are chronically feeling lonely, depressed or unhappy; if you have no joy or motivations in your life do *not* think for one moment that having a baby will solve your problems. Quite the contrary, the event will only serve to worsen your situation. If this is sounds like you, seek psychological help. Talking to a trained professional will help you to ease and work through your anxieties. It will help you to process and get over whatever it is that has happened to you in your life. An unprocessed trauma is like poorly digested food—it's uncomfortable and upsetting and needs a good remedy. With time on your side, and if you are able to overcome your inner conflicts, you will be in much better condition emotionally to embrace motherhood. You should think deeply about these matters. If you haven't been able to resolve the conflicts of your past, you will not be able to meet your child's basic needs.

According to psychologist Abraham Maslow, every human being has two kinds of needs—basic needs and developmental needs. The first group includes the need for love, respect, self-esteem, safety and commitment, which are critically important for the human soul, just as water, amino acids, proteins and calcium are for the body. These are referred to as *deficit* needs because they can only be satisfied from outside ourselves, from that one indispensable mother figure during babyhood and early childhood. We cannot fill these deficits from within ourselves. And, if they are absent, we cannot be motivated to develop the second group of needs, namely, our own potential and inclinations, the choice of our mission in life, our destiny or our calling. Sometimes, when faced with such privations, a woman will want to have a child, thus creating a situation by which she hopes to fill the emptiness she feels, trying to give herself what has remained unsatisfied within.

A person's adult life unfolds differently when his or her basic needs have been met and not when it is motivated by an incessant search to remedy the frustrations and privations of one's early years. Bad relationships, addictions, compulsive shopping, having an abusive partner—all these lead to our trying to fill in feelings of emptiness at the expense of our own health and emotional well-being.

The right time to become a mother

At what point in your life should you consider becoming a mom? Let's dwell on this a little and go deeper into the matter. The following three-step guide will provide you with some answers.

1) The first step is to know whether or not you are prepared for motherhood, whether or not you have been able to develop the maternal instinct or perhaps you are simply moved by the instinct to reproduce. There is no obligation to have a baby, but confusing motivations may lead you to think otherwise. To begin with, in our uncaring culture we look at the female biological clock which tells us we are old at age 40. Or, perhaps, your own mother was a suffocating parent, and now you— for emotional reasons—need to prove that you can be a better mother than she was. Or perhaps you suffered from neglect and need to compensate for the family you never had by creating one of your own. I remember the case of a young woman living with a male partner who had to work day and night in order to make ends meet. At one point she became quite concerned about irregularities in her menstrual cycle. When she was asked, Could it be that you're pregnant? She replied with a smile of delight, "God, I hope so!" What would become of a child born under such circumstances, with his struggling parents away from home, and no one to properly look after and nurture him? Ponder these things, and make your own story a good one by

thinking deeply about your early life and your present circumstances. Think about the reasons that motivate you to want that pregnancy. Talk to a friend, a priest or a psychologist, someone whose hand you can hold, to help you achieve what you really want and not what your life may have pushed you into choosing.

2) The second step involves being legally bound to the man you love—a man who is ready and prepared to be a father. Married or single is not the same. A couple's marital status is very important when contemplating bringing up a child. Of course love is essential, and just having certain legal papers is no guarantee of happiness; having them, however does guarantee your child's basic self-esteem when at school, when comparing himself with his friends and not being an object of discrimination. To have a partner without any binding legal documents is acceptable only if your idea is to live out a romance. But when it comes to family, you must legalize the bond for the sake of your child's status in society and before God, if that applies. You must understand that on becoming a mother your personal projects are no longer part of the equation. Your needs must be balanced and include giving priority to your infant child.

You might say to me, "That's old-fashioned." Well, consider this: One of the causes of the breakdown of family life is the abandonment of this old-fashioned idea to the self-centeredness of today's parents. Family is the core of any healthy society. Feminist movements have contributed significantly to a breakdown of the family in their struggle to achieve gender equality. But, unlike motherhood, gender roles is a cultural construct and, in terms of family and children, has brought about substantial imbalances in modern-day societies with men and women being considered as one and the same, without ostensible differences, without sex-specific characteristics.

In such androgynous societies both partners in a marriage get up early to go to work and earn money, with one partner perhaps earning more than the other—incidentally having a sexual relationship. However, when babies come along, the task of providing must go to the male, and the momentary reproductive role to the female. The couple—male and female—presides over the human family just as nature rules over day and night. Hot-cold, high tide-low tide. They are the two faces of the same coin, complementing each other, ensuring balance in the universe. Gender equality will only be possible when we learn to respect the complementary differences between men and women—those differences that tend to bring us together rather than into head-on confrontations. If you're a feminist, think of it this way: Equality within differences.

3) Finally, financial stability is a must if the mother is to give priority to her child during the first six years of his life. What do I mean by this? I mean her being with the child most of the time during this crucial period

in the shaping of his human psyche. Our adult personality is the product of seeds planted during the critical years of our early life. In fact, early emotional lessons and experiences tend to deepen and flourish later during puberty. Nothing you do or teach after that time has passed will change what was absorbed and learned earlier by your child. In order for this process to be a success, you will need firm support from your partner to enable you to monitor your offspring's development. Of course you can work or study online at home. By organizing your life in this way you will be able to provide your child with essential dosages of frustration which, in small amounts, like vaccines, are crucial to his well-being. However, don't go overboard on this. The child must still come first. Keep in mind, it is one thing to over-indulge the child and another to provide him with what is essential. If you do the right thing, you and your child will be on the slow road to autonomy from each other and your own horizons will begin to open up before you. Don't rush your decision-making. Don't look around to see what others are doing. Don't copy what they do. Wait, and prepare yourself, and then enter into motherhood having the necessary basic support. Let us now consider the reasons.

CHAPTER III

THE BIRTH OF YOUR CHILD AND THE GRANDMOTHER'S ROLE IN HIS LIFE

Your baby's birthing experience

Certainly, the slow road to adult independence is strewn with significant milestones—unforgettable moments filled with responsible love—stages facilitated by the consistent and loving presence of the mother—a mother who understands the vicissitudes her baby is undergoing in this first stage just after birth. *The mother* surrenders her narcissism for the sake of the child. It is a surrendering that begins in her womb—a magic cauldron from which the epic that is life emerges. The womb is an earthly paradise, an unrestricted shelter of protection and nurturing. Inside it, your child will undergo his first exile, his first goodbye and his first disappointment, and will have a sampling of all the losses and grief he will face throughout his life. Pay attention.

To fully imagine the helplessness your baby feels before, during and after the birthing process is nearly impossible for you, or for any woman, because in this crucial process, all we can think about is the pain we are enduring. All the mother can think of is how much pain she can withstand or how much harder she must push. But what is the newborn going through?

The following imprecise but valid metaphor will help you understand roughly the feelings of helplessness and distress your baby experiences during the birthing process.

Just try to imagine yourself asleep in your warm, soft bed on a frigid winter night, the warm atmosphere and the last sounds you heard blending in with your dreams. How great it feels! It's one of those nights when you feel like sleeping in. No noises, no disruptions. You are lulled by the promise of a steaming cup of coffee in the morning. But, after a few hours, something strange interrupts your sleep—a change of temperature and bodily sensations. Then you wake up naked on frozen ground, shivering. You hear distant voices muttering in a strange language. You perceive ghostly figures, but can't see or hear too much. Someone holds you firmly and lifts you up—big hands, strong arms. And there you are, weak and helpless, shivering and squirming. The strange sensations increase—there is a kind of intense pressure in your chest. Your lungs fill with air for the first time. You breathe. Your cries soon turn into wailing. Your body stirs, unable to coordinate any effective movement or motion. You feel only uncaring abandonment. You want to get back into that bed, back into the warmth. But you cannot. You are trapped in a real, living nightmare.

When you are newly born, the only thing that can comfort you in the midst of all this chaos, are the tender arms and the unmistakable aroma of your mother—the soft bed to which you return. Her warm milk nourishes you and gives you your first feeling of satisfaction, of shelter and calmness—the feeling that you will never be left alone.

Crying is the only recourse which nature has given to human infants. They are not endowed with the instinct of self-preservation; hence physical and emotional attachment to the mother is their only assurance of survival.

Emotional bonding with the mother is extraordinarily powerful during this time, and the series of interactions taking place between the infant and the mother will have benefits for both. Exactly what am I referring to and why do I say that a nanny cannot replace the mother? In the birthing process, the mother's body releases powerful hormones that help her to create an intimate bond with her baby, among them is oxytocin, the so-called "love hormone." Yes. Let's be clear; a mother must be in love with her baby so she can give herself over to him. This should not be misunderstood. It's a kind of "chemical love" bestowed by nature during the very first month of the newborn to assure the continuation of the species. It is a love that transforms itself into healing substances that benefit your baby. If you have learned to develop a strong maternal instinct, you're in optimal condition to make use of these substances to provide your offspring with the best possible prescription for his or her health. So, the intense anxiety that your little one feels due to the birthing trauma will be absorbed by you as you keep him calm with caresses and assure him that all is well. If this specific and special pacifying relationship does not take place, the infant will grow up having difficulty in forming intimate and emotionally healthy relationships. It will be difficult for him or her to learn, to work, to love or to have children. The more you caress your infant and tell him that you love him, the fewer illnesses he will suffer from, and the friendlier and more compassionate he will be toward others. Of course, in order to achieve this, you must hold firm to the belief that nothing is more important to you than your child during the early years of his life. It is a mutual molding process by which mother and child beneficially influence each other. Only you, Mom, can understand your infant's physical needs. Why this is so, we don't fully understand, but it is true. Only you wake up to the cry of your child, yet sleep through other louder noises. Only you can tell early on when a fever is in progress.

Communication between mother and child at this stage is completely intuitive. Beginning with pre-verbal communication, the infant gradually progresses from *receiving* signals from inside his own body (temperature, sleepiness, hunger, pain) which is called the "*reception phase*" to *receiving* signals from outside himself via the sense organs (sight, hearing, smell, touch and taste) which is called the "*perception phase*".

So, as you can see, *perception* is something that is barely developed in the newborn. On the other hand, *reception* has developed to a much greater degree and is more reliable even than it is in adults because it helps the infant to survive through his mother. It is dialogue without language or gestures and it is immediate and intuitive. But if the infant perceives that you are pulling back, he will react to your rejection. Oftentimes he will become sick or anxious and will have difficulty sleeping. Inexplicably, he will sense your desperation to get back to your job or get back to your normal weight, for example. This is a bad start for his tender life—a life in which he must now exert himself to "seduce" his unhappy mother whose pregnancy might have been an accident or perhaps had her baby for the wrong reasons.

Upon a child's reaching school age, a slow process of mutual independence and emotional re-adaptation begins to take place—one that started long ago, in small cost-free doses without any needless losses. It is definitely not a good idea to prematurely break the branch from off the tree. Let us reflect further on these matters.

The importance of the emotional colostrum
Your child was inside you. He knows your aroma, the rhythm of your heart, the distant sound of your

soothing words—sounds that reverberate within him. It is all familiar to him. Have you noticed how he calms down when lying on your bosom? Gradually, because of this attachment, and not being constantly handed over to another person, a dim consciousness of reality begins to slowly emerge for him. If he is deprived of this consistent attention and is missing the tonality of your voice, the infant will evolve anyway, no doubt, but he or she will be flawed. In your own past, in your college years, did you ever experience a constant substitution of professors? I offer this weak and inadequate analogy with the aim of drawing an imprecise comparison. After getting used to a professor's way of explaining things, to his pauses and ways of summing up, in comes a replacement and you are forced to adapt. I have known people who, because of their jobs, have to move several times a year. If we shift these fragile comparisons to the gamut of the needs a helpless baby who is beset by internal tensions that he cannot process—the consequences can be very damaging. You, at least, have reached adulthood. You have a "self," a personality. Perhaps you still don't know exactly who you are or what you expect from life, but you do have some understanding of reality, and hopefully you have defenses against anxiety and loss. You have language with which to express your anger which you can alleviate through the words you use. The infant has only you, his mother, to signify his reality. He can't be constantly handed over to different people, because if this happens, he will always be going back to the starting point. Moreover, no one can cuddle your child better than you. And only you can determine your child's emotional state; by this I mean only you can understand your child's moods and empathize with him. This is what I call the *emotional colostrum*, which, just as in the case of breast milk, is something like a valuable, free vaccine, the effects of which last throughout your child's life. You should not withhold the flow of this "psychological breast milk" too soon, nor should you prolong it unnecessarily. The watchword is that you should neither indulge your child nor abandon him. Moderation and balance are the keys.

It is not that you need to spend the entire day physically bonded to your child. I heard one young woman complain, "There's no day off for me!" Your infant should know that you are right there and available, but not "glued" to him. He needs to count on your presence-absence, so that he knows you are close by to meet his needs—in a nearby room, say, the living room. And he should learn, gradually, to sleep in his own bed. Some children adapt more quickly than others. Analyze and observe your young child.

The yearning to be someone in life arises out of a deficiency, from a feeling of incompleteness, that something is lacking, and this is a healthy feeling. I do not mean not providing for your child's basic needs nor being absent from the home during the first six years of his life. Balance is the key—knowing what to provide and what to withhold. This is why you should try to establish a healthy medium which you can later adjust according your child's desire for gifts or outings. The byword is *neither too little nor too much*—to avoid excesses—the *hubris* talked about by the Greeks.

We conclude, then that, in addition to meeting the child's basic needs described above, he must have an attentive mother close at hand rather than some substitute or "primary caregiver", as they say nowadays.

The role of the grandmother

At this point, you, young mom, are feeling happy because your own mother looks after your little one while you hold down a full-time job. But, I would like to go into this matter a bit deeper. Those of us who are grandmothers should not be given the responsibility of raising our grandchildren; although, of course, we can be a great help when they are sick or when the parents are on holiday, which is not that often. Note that, we grandmothers' biological clocks stopped long ago. Everything we do when looking after our grandchildren we do from our heart, out of pure love and raw effort. We have already raised our families and put forth a lot of effort in the process. Now it's time to enjoy the grandchildren as family on weekends, to give them advice guidance, to visit with them and play with them—to cook some delicious favorite recipe. Now it's time for us grandmothers—time to enjoy, time to live out our long-delayed dreams because when we were much younger, you, dear children, came first.

Motherhood, dear female friend, is a non-transferable state—a responsibility. Remember, *to become a mother is not a destination but a conscious decision.* Author Antonio Guijarro wrote an excellent book entitled "The Slave Grandmother Syndrome" which I recommend to you. It is about the abuse of grandmothers in capitalist societies. I'm not saying that you are guilty of doing this. But it is something to think about. No matter how much experience a grandmother has had and no matter how much she wishes to help out, raising a child, dear friend, is *your* sacred duty. So, think twice. If you don't agree, then you shouldn't have children. Why am I so insistent on this point? Why do I stress in particular the paradox of conceiving a life and then delegating its upbringing to the care of a nanny or grandmother? The contradiction is too obvious to any woman who will open her eyes.

For what reason, mother-friend, would you want to deprive yourself of the gratifying sacrifice of motherhood; of the sweet burden of the long hours of parenting where fatigue is mixed with the satisfaction of watching your child grow and change minute by minute? Be proud of yourself! You are the special biological helper of your child; you are his walking stick and sole helper during the first years of his life, someone to accompany him during the whole process that will take him from total dependency to adult independence—a process that will transform him into a well-adapted, sociable, mature human being. Everything we become as adults is the outcome of all that we have experienced during the first six years of our existence. Of this I am absolutely convinced. It is not by chance that schooling begins around this time. However, in recent decades, the age for entry into school has changed drastically. While the cycle of primary education begins at age 6, in capitalist societies, a new phenomenon has emerged with a vengeance. It is the phenomenon of nurseries or what we could call "*mothergartens*" intended for infants from 0 to 3 years of age. We want to separate ourselves from our children right after they are born so we can go back to work and make money. The assistance provided at such nurseries is not always of the best quality, and those with the highest standards require a budget that few families can afford.

Ignoring these risks and leaving an infant in the care of others at such a tender age means forcing adjustments on him, forcing him to evolve much too quickly. Such a false and fragile equilibrium can break down at any moment. If a mother is not with her child for the crucial length of time, he will become self-sufficient at some point, but such independence will be premature and will have the consequence of creating a *false self* in the child—one who resembles—but is not—an adult.

Sooner or later he or she will regress to try to recover the missing phase in his or her life, but by then it will be too late. There is a Spanish cartoon called *Don Fulgencio* which portrays the goings-on of a man without a childhood—a laughable businessman acting out childlike behavior. We must be aware that in nature everything needs time to mature and take place: a pregnancy, the earth as it orbits the sun and rotates on its own axis, the changing seasons, etc. During the first six years of a human life, especially the first 36 months, there are milestones and turning points in the psychophysical development of the infant that he cannot successfully arrive at without the loving presence of a mother and the altruistic cooperation of a father—one who, with neither jealousy nor reproaches, allows his wife to dedicate herself almost exclusively to the care of their child. These milestones in the child's psychological development unfold in three stages described by Dr. Margaret Mahler, the Austro-Hungarian psychoanalyst pediatrician and specialist in child psychology. I cite this professional because of her detailed descriptions of a mother's monumental task during this developmental process.

The next section contains a synthesis and an approximation of a body of essential and multi-layered knowledge which I believe should be shared with prospective parents from a teaching platform that I call *The University of the Family.*

CHAPTER IV

YOUR INFANT'S PSYCHOLOGICAL DEVELOPMENT. THE FIRST 36 MONTHS

Margaret Mahler states that human psychological development occurs in two stages, each different from the other, yet interrelated, namely, *biological birth and psychological birth*. These two phases, she explains, take place at different times. The first is an observable and spectacular event around the birth of a child which takes place on the boundary between the final weeks of pregnancy and the infant's first month of life on the outside.

The second phase is a slow developmental process that takes place in the psyche of the newborn, whose main achievements occur between five months and three years of age. During this period, the infant begins to acquire its individuality and identity in a gradual physical separation from the mother. However, bear in mind that this stage endures throughout the life of an individual. Its reverberations can be seen in behaviors displayed during new and different phases of our life's cycles—adolescence, adulthood, menopause, andropause and old age—in which behaviors originating from the learnings of our earliest childhood come to the surface. It is an outstanding case in point of the extreme importance of an infant's relationship to his or her mother during life's early years.

Biological birth

This consists of two sub-phases: normal autism and natural symbiosis.

Normal autism

You may be surprised to learn that, indeed, there is such a thing as normal autism. It occurs during the last weeks of pregnancy and the first month of the infant's life outside the uterus. It is defined as a body-centered state. Etymologically, the word "autism" means withdrawal from oneself. It is a state similar to life inside the womb. As previously explained, a baby is totally open to internal stimuli (sensations of hunger, sleepiness, thirst, etc.) but virtually closed to those coming from outside himself. He does not recognize his mother or his surroundings. This condition is a protective mechanism intended for his survival. It is an encapsulating maneuver that protects him from what feels like harmful forces coming from outside himself. The image of a turtle illustrates this. Your baby is hypersensitive to anything that happens outside himself; therefore biology provides him with a strong anti-stimulus barrier that prevents him from exiting his "shell." Therefore, he cannot distinguish between what is outside and his internal world, between animate or inanimate things. A newborn infant is an entirely biological organism. He is the repository of internal tensions that need to be released in order for him to maintain his organic balance. He does this by vomiting, writhing, crying—behaviors that prevail during the first weeks of his life. He is not aware of the mother who holds him, calms him and feeds him, she who meets his basic needs. To this infant, the breast that feeds him is part of his own organic cycles and not something separate from himself. So you think to yourself, "If this baby doesn't recognize me as his mother, then what difference does it make if I nurse him or someone else does?" Careful! This is simply not the case. Re-read and think about the previous chapters.

NORMAL AUTISM

You might be curious to understand the difference between normal and pathological autism. I shall explain. Pathological autism is a developmental disorder caused by some kind of disturbance during the stage of normal autism. The infant finds himself in this autistic sub-phase during the first month of life and remains in this state. He is not capable of recognizing his mother or his surroundings. There is a "wall of remoteness" between the autistic infant and the outside world. This anti-external stimuli barrier seems to stay put. There are many reasons for this—abnormal brain chemistry, hormonal deficiencies, emotional stress and environmental factors. According to some psychologists, autism in infants has been attributed to early physical abuse by the parents. It has also been attributed to painful medical procedures. Psychologist René Spitz writes about infants who are separated from their mothers very early on. And there is the opposite phenomena, such when the mother is pathologically too attached to her child. Remember the watchword: "moderation."

In deep pathological autism, the child refuses to be separated from his mother and denies the existence of the outside world. Remember, that *to recognize the mother as an "other" is a precondition for recognizing other people and for opening up to life.* People talk about the autistic child's lack of empathy. This happens in autistic children because the amygdala, located in the area of the brain where emotions and the ability to empathize, does not function properly. Nor do such children have the ability to recognize signs of sadness, joy or worry in the faces of others.

It should be pointed out that autism is not a disease but an array of anomalies—signs and symptoms that impede a child's social development. That is why it is called ASD, (autistic syndrome) which has many gradations, from severe autism, already summarized, to a high-functioning autism which experts sometimes refer to as Asperger Syndrome.

Reference: In autism, the term *sign*, is used to describe an array of behaviors, for example when a child is called by his or her name and does not respond. In autism the term *symptom*, means for instance, a child who is absolutely unable to communicate or interact with anyone.

Normal symbiosis

What does the term *symbiosis* mean? This word has been borrowed from biology. In the animal world a symbiotic relationship is one in which two species benefit from each other; for example, the cowherd bird feeds on the ticks on a cow's back. In this situation, the cow gets free tick removal and the bird gets its nourishment. Symbiosis is the most important force for mutual aid on earth, as it promotes cooperation for the formation of new social groups. In the symbiotic bond between mother and child, the child benefits by getting adequate nourishment and care, and the mother is given the opportunity to "extend" gestation outside the womb. For the infant, the symbiotic phase begins to emerge around the end of the fifth month of life when it slowly begins to have an awareness of the world outside itself. However, it is not yet able to face or adapt to that world. It has not yet developed a *self*, that is, it has not acquired the necessary "database" that includes rules, defenses, values and ideals. The *self* of the infant is still inadequate for it to survive on its own. Unfortunately, as human beings, our instinct for conservation is atrophied. That is why nature has given us Mothers. Empathy coming from a mother, obviously having learned the maternal instinct, replaces for us human beings, the instincts on which some animals totally depend for their survival. Empathy, as we stated earlier, means the ability to be in someone else's shoes— that is, to put ourselves in their place. The mother puts herself in her baby's place and begins to play the role of something like an *auxiliary self*. She relieves her infant's tensions and needs because she feels them as her own. She is moved; that is, she moves with the rhythms of her baby.

The psycho-biological bonding between mother and child, at this stage, rounds out the infant's precarious self. This relationship between mother and child is called the *maternal dyad*. It is a state of mutual interdependence in which mother and child communicate with each other by way of signals, signs, gestures and postures in a climate of affection involving warm, repetitious tenderness. It is pre-verbal communication, similar in many respects to the ways in which animals communicate.

NORMAL SIMBIOSIS

Experts point out that communication among animals is egocentric; that is, it is centered on the subject and not on the receiver, which would be *allocentric* social communication. When a horse whinnies it is not trying to send a message; it is simply responding reflexively to a stimulus. Human beings have inherited this animal-egocentric means of communication as part of our phylogenetic makeup. And infants use it in the early months of their lives. Later, if a child's personality develops in a healthy way, he will willingly and consciously avail himself of *allocentric* language in communicating with others. The culmination of this process will be the acquisition of speech which is also referred to as the *symbolic function* because, clearly, words are symbols representing things or actions. Some might claim that in maternal symbiosis communication is an extrasensory or telepathic condition, but this can't be proven. In this symbiosis, the mother does not register in the child's mind as being separate from himself. Although similar to normal autism, it differs, however, in that in the case of normal autism there is no mother-infant communication because the baby does not register the mother's existence. A *dyad* is characterized by mutual exchanges and influences between baby and mother. I will go into how they communicate at both stages.

Freud, in his magnificent book *Project for a Scientific Psychology* (1895) discusses the nature of communication in the *dyad*. When faced with an internal need such as hunger, the infant cries to express emotion related to this need but cannot go in search of his food. His crying attracts his mother's attention and she responds by feeding him. Freud called this reaction the infant's "satisfaction experience" thanks to help given to him from the outside, called motherly care.

Pathological symbiosis

As in the case of autism, symbiosis can also be pathological. In this case, an infant is in the normal symbiosis stage with the mother, but in a distorted way. He continues to perceive the mother as being part of himself, as though merged with her and this normal symbiosis phase is prolonged and the infant's psychological birth does not take place. If this phase is not completed the infant will not attain the independence he needs to enable him to develop normally. Some experts consider such a situation as a kind of secondary autism.

Let us now take a look at the second stage of an infant's psychological development. It is a defining moment because it is the fundamental separation of the child from his mother leading to his own individuality and to having relationships with others besides his mother.

Psychological birth

Separation

The end of the infant's fifth month marks the end of his symbiotic bonding with the mother. The shell is broken, so to speak. The extra-uterine pregnancy has come to an end. This is the point where the infant is born *psychologically* and the beginning of *separation-individuation*. These are two separate but closely inter-connected events. At this stage the infant begins to understand his mother's separateness and his own limits. Little by little, he begins to discover the world around him, and his mother. He is responsive and alert to the voices and sounds of his environment in the same way he was previously responsive to stimuli from within his own body. He begins to rehearse his future freedom and independence from the first object of love for both boys and girls—Mom.

Individuation

The end of the infant's fifth month marks the end of his symbiotic bonding with the mother. The shell is broken, so to speak. The extra-uterine pregnancy has come to an end. This is the point where the infant is born psychologically and the beginning of separation-individuation. These are two separate but closely inter-connected events. At this stage the infant begins to understand his mother's separateness and his own limits. Little by little, he begins to discover the world around him, and his mother. He is responsive and alert to the voices and sounds of his environment in the same way he was previously responsive to stimuli from within his own body. He begins to rehearse his future freedom and independence from the first object of love for both boys and girls—Mom.

Individuación

Individuation has to do with the development of the EGO and cognitive skills. What do I mean by the term EGO? In colloquial language it is defined as "exaggerated self-esteem." We say, He is a selfish or egocentric person. However, from the point of view of psychology, EGO is an instance or site of the psyche by which a person recognizes himself as well as others—a self who shares life with other different selves. So, what is the psyche? The psyche is the mixture of the processes that make up the human mind. It is what allows

one to distinguish his or her distinct and unique individuality, to be happy and achieve goals without
harming anyone else by accepting society's rules and
parameters.

Cognitive skills are those skills that facilitate knowledge; attention, memory, processing, all of which begin
at this stage.

SEPARATION-INDIVIDUATION
PSYCHOLOGICAL BIRTH

The high point of this period of separation-individuation is reached when the infant is able to internalize
his mother. What does this mean? It is a psychological process by which the infant in his psyche inter-
nalizes the image of his mother. He absorbs her image
and behaviors as one absorbs food. Hence, the mother
becomes a protective shield that will enable her child
to face difficult situations in his life with confidence
and a high degree of self-esteem. If this psychological

internalization of the mother is missing, it can be the cause of a child's chronic insecurities and basic low self-esteem.

Overall, if separation-individuation does not take place a child, upon reaching adulthood, will have great difficulty in maintaining a sense of his or her own identity and will possibly have an out-of-balance EGO that can lead to the well-known condition of exaggerated self-esteem or self-love, or possibly to having a weak and undefined EGO.

CHAPTER V

FROM THE BABY'S FIFTH MONTH ONWARD: LEARNING VALUES, LIMITS AND ACQUIRING CAPACITIES

Mom's face - a mirror of the world

At around the fifth month of life, changes will occur in the psyche of your infant that are of vital importance to his cognitive and social development—a number of responses to incentives coming from the outside. His first response is a smile. A dawning of reality begins to occur in your baby through this first sign. That is, he recognizes external stimuli to which he responds while at the same time temporarily suspending the *pleasure principle*, identified by Freud, that requires exclusive attention to his physical needs.

The smile, which appears while looking directly at any moving face, is the visible expression of a particular way of developing the child's psyche. In short, your baby is capable of responding with a smile to a particular stimulus—namely, that of a moving, smiling face that is looking directly at him or her. To the infant, it's not Mom's face, yet. At this point, you can even show him the moving face of a monster and he will smile, provided these two conditions are met: facing him and in motion. A SIDE VIEW WILL NOT WORK. As it is still not Mom's face, this stage is called the "precursor object stage." Don't panic if this doesn't make sense. I will explain. You, Mom, are the object. It means that he is developing the conditions so that, at around eight months, he will smile only when he sees your face, Mom, whereas an unfamiliar face will cause him distress. That is why this phenomenon is known as "eighth-month anguish." Mom is now for the first time the object of his love, recognized and valued. Eureka!

During the precursor stage, a higher organization of the psyche occurs that did not previously exist. In this case, if the child smiles when he sees a face with certain characteristics it is because somehow he remembers that sign. The existence of memory implies the beginning of a division within his psyche that was not there previously. Consequently, it is the beginning of elemental or basic thinking and memory.

The workings of a baby's psyche

A baby's psyche is comparable to a screen on which no movie has yet been projected. At around the 5th month, the infant's relationship with his mother induces the projection of the very first images on his psyche—those of the mother. These precursors of memory and representations, and all later thoughts, are related to Mom. How does this happen? When you distance yourself from him, you gradually let him develop his earliest memories—memories of you, of your face, of your aroma. Sometimes you are not there; this means that you start leaving him alone at certain times, for example, he wakes up from a nap, and you're not in the room. Or when he is left with Grandma because you have a doctor's appointment or some work to do. His extreme anxiety to see you will release within him a primitive mental representation of your image, and it will console him. This mechanism provides the basis for what in psychology is known as the "*secondary process*" which is indispensable for the rest of our lives. Through this process we calm our hunger pangs while thinking of a pizza and waiting for someone to bring it. We learn to postpone desires, to control them and to learn that things are not always "*right away*" or "*here and now.*" This is how the infant's psyche begins to accumulate memories based on primordial images—yours, Mom—so that when you go away for a few moments you allow him to remember you, and this remembering calms the distress caused by your absence. Individuals who have not successfully completed this stage, who did not learn to wait, are prey to their impulses, to an emotional loss of control that leads them to committing wrongdoings in order to fulfill their desires. People who cheat, kill, or gamble away their earnings, are usually those who did not experience this supremely important psychological and human process. By this same process your child will know that if he wants to have a sports car he will have to work and earn money in order to buy it and not go out and steal it.

It is not only you, buddy-Mom, who facilitates the development of the thinking and memory processes in your child, but your face, undoubtedly, will be the first mirror through which he will learn to recognize his own moods: joy or sadness, concern or anger. By your gestures he will know whether or not he is accepted or rejected. He will learn what he can become in life. As Aristotle once said, at birth we are all *tabula rasa* or blank slates. We did not show up with a script in hand. It is for this reason that we as parents must transmit a way of living life.

Piera Aulagnier, a German psychoanalyst uses the term *"primary violence"*—a necessary transfer of parental culture to their children, a roadmap. The crux of the matter is to know where to stop, so as not to fall into what she calls *"secondary violence"* because there will come a point at which a child must choose his own destiny, draw his own roadmap.

The above makes it clear that a mother's face is the first mirror seen by the infant child. Through her facial expressions and gestures of approval or displeasure, the child discovers his own different emotional states.

Your baby discovers himself in the mirror

Sometime between the baby's 6th and 18th month, there occurs in his neuro-psychological development what French psychoanalyst Jackes Lacan calls the *mirror stage*. The infant, accustomed to deducing his moods from his mother's face will later see and discover the image of his entire body in the mirrors found around the house. Such moments of discovery are critical milestones in an infant's evolution. The young infant's extreme neurological immaturity prevents him from being able to recognize his own body, much less being able to move it at his bidding. He is only able to sees some parts of his body in motion—a hand, a foot. Only when Mom places him in front of a mirror does this foundational moment of human experience occur. In addition to discovering his own body in the mirror, celebrated with joy, he hears his mother's words telling him how beautiful he is as she envisages a wonderful future for him. He will become a doctor like his uncle Albert. He will become a great financier like his grandfather, etc., etc. We tell our children of our expectations as a guide for their lives.

This emotional exercise is an early application of the power of words which is crucial to the development of life as an adult. A gesture of confirmation tells him: *that means you*, as he looks at you and smiles, while vigorously kicking. At such moments, there arises a vague awareness of bodily integrity; things start to make sense—the image of his entire little body that he sees in the mirror which he had not previously recognized. It is he, himself. Previously he discerned only parts of his body; now he sees all of it. It is his first experience of human totality, holistic and of supreme importance. In short, we are a *self*, consisting primarily of a human body—a place from which our human experience is registered. But, it is not only the discovery of the body. The infant's image of his body is supported, now, by words that sustain him and give him life as a human being—Mom's words.

In animals this significant process does not happen in the same way. A fledgling just needs to see another fledgling in order for its sexual cells to mature. In humans, maturation takes place only if and when the bodily image is accompanied by maternal words that connote it and give it meaning. And here we must pay attention. The power of words is magical and transcendent, because by their influence we make those we love fortunate or happy, wise or ignorant. We can influence, manipulate or provide relief. We can raise children who are either free or repressed, sure of themselves or vulnerable. If you tell your child he is useless, that is what he will become. Similarly, if you inspire him with words of encouragement he will become successful and happy if you keep his self-esteem high.

From the child's 36th month onward, and provided the previous phases have been completed satisfactorily, he will be able to separate himself from you and show the beginnings of his independence. At this stage the child is able to introduce himself into society on his own. With his embryonic personality he expresses both aversion and pleasure. He becomes a great explorer of his world and of words. His eyes roam and dare to discover things. He is eager to reach out and to learn. He observes his mother while crawling around or taking his first steps away from her, more and more frequently. He begins to affirm himself. However, after age two a series of actions on the part of the mother take place designed to help him overcome his fears and to have his first encounter with the value of limits.

The efficacy of *No*

No starts when your infant is in his earliest days. It promotes health and development. By two years of age or earlier the child is walking and touching everything. He starts misbehaving, breaking things. You, the Mom, start increasing the *Don'ts—Don't touch that, Don't go there, etc.* These *No*'s are emotionally frustrating for the child because they hinder him from doing what he wants to do. You frustrate him, and that frustration generates in him aggression towards you. The relationship, therefore, starts to become ambivalent. Before, he loved you; now he dislikes you because you prevent him from doing what he wants to do. At this stage, he begins to shake his head in a semantic gesture of denial. He copies you, identifies with you. Now it is he who says *No*. His *No*'s are his resistance to frustration and set the stage for the typical stubbornness of the second year of a child's life. By identifying with his mother means not losing her as an object of love. It means identifying himself with what is an early prohibition—a responsibility the father will assume later. The mother teaches the limits within the home and family. The father will teach him culture's protocols—prohibitions that will serve him well for living in society.

No is beneficial. It gives us wings. It is like a lubricant for our relationships with our peers in the world, because we respect them, because we give them their space. *No* has the value of setting limits. These *No's* are like tracks on which the train of a child's life circulates, which will prevent him from derailing.

Fear of the dark

Fear of the dark is part of the human evolutionary process. It is a natural defensive reaction. Primitive man feared nocturnal predators that menaced him because he couldn't see who or what they were. Fear forced him to hide to avoid falling prey to them. Somehow we have inherited this ancestral fear, which is expressed more intensely in a child's early years.

Fear of the dark appears at around two years of age and continues up to age eight or nine. There are precedents, since in general this fear gradually grows as the imagination of the child grows. For example, at eight months he is afraid when he sees a strange face because he is looking for his mother's face. At two years of age he feels fear of abandonment if you leave him at the nursery or with Grandma; and at age four he starts becoming afraid of the dark. He may also begin to fear animals. Other fears and insecurities appear at around age six.

What to do if your child is particularly susceptible to these fears at bedtime? Do not intimidate him by making him go to his room or go to bed if he misbehaves. His bedroom should not be connected with punishment. Don't make him feel that you desperately want him to go the bed so you can watch TV or be alone. Be patient. Play with him for a few minutes after dinner, perhaps some game that soothes him. Sing him a soft lullaby; read him a story that doesn't have witches or evil characters. Install a dim light in his room that doesn't cast shadows on the wall. Remember, his imagination now creates ghosts that did not exist before. If he is still afraid, take him by the hand and wait for him to go to sleep. Let him hug his teddy bear, a toy or a piece of cloth. Oftentimes his pacifier will do the trick. Next we will discuss the importance of these toys and pieces of cloth.

The meaning of your child's favorite toy

Along the road leading to independence and to life in society, toys and objects facilitate this transition. Hence they are called *transitionals*. The teddy bear, a piece of cloth or a pacifier are objects that infants want and are grateful for. Their absence can bring them heartbreak. These precious talismans facilitate their separation from the mother which gradually begins at this stage. That is why it is practically impossible to take these objects away from the child while he is taking pleasure in them, especially at night. Mom goes away but teddy bear stays. This is how he is able to accept her absence. It is crucial to allow him these initial attachments which psychologist Winnicott refers to as *transitional objects*. This refers to objects that allow us to journey from our mother's bosom into the world, into adult life where our Mom-friend will not always be present. They are bridges and there is a normal mourning period whereby the child gradually accepts the absence of the mother.

What is the right moment to take away these meaningful items, especially the pacifier? If your child has been properly raised, understood and encouraged, there will be no need to use force to remove these items as has been done in the past. I remember how our family doctor flung my pacifier out the window. It is unusual for me to be able to remember this, as I was just an infant. In my mind I remember Dr. Viglino doing what he, at the time, deemed beneficial for my development. With absolute goodwill and unawareness, the doctor prevented the process from resolving itself naturally, as he should have. At some point the child will cast the pacifier aside. My daughter, Barbara, who is 30 at the time of this writing, at around 18 months, suddenly threw away her pacifier, saying, Yuck!

Mom, the great transformer

Psychologist Christopher Bollas referred to the mother as the *transformational object*—she who will transform her baby into an independent and happy being; she who helps him in the slow process of separation-individuation; in his becoming separate from you; in distancing himself to become a distinct individual, strong and self-realized; someone without crutches; someone who loves and respects himself while loving and respecting others. You are the facilitator of this process. You, with your care and caresses, continually affect your child's environment. You bathe him, you talk to him. You change his diaper. You develop his motor skills through playing with him. These changes in his environment produce other internal changes that will affect the development of his mind. In you, your baby finds love and security; in the way you lull him to sleep; in the way you hold him. And he grows internally as well. That is why it is so important that you alone be the one who cares for him, even though he still doesn't recognize you as his mother, but only lives through you and experiences though you. By living through you he can take in your mental state, your moods. If a child does not have a transformative mother he or she could become prey to psychological problems.

Note that in extreme cases, such as when a baby is abandoned by his mother, he may die from what is known as "hospitalism" or "anaclitic depression." This happens to babies who have initially been cared for and then abandoned in hospitals. Although they are fed by attentive nurses, they end up dying in the absence of that personal intimacy with the mother. You, the mother, are for him a genuine "auxiliary self" during the period in which his own "self" has not yet developed. Tenderly, you give to him, provide for him, and pass on to him the rules of life. It is a temporary phase, of course. Later on he will develop his wings. He will create his own experiences. He will take wing in the certainty that no turbulence will bring him down.

What are the counsels that parents can follow with regard to their infant at this stage of his life? Let's look into the matter.

Fewer electronics and more conversation

Be aware that even during the first few months of a baby's life, the family PC or laptop may be in a common place in the house, accessible to the entire family, such as the living room. You should accustom your child to the fact that his own room and the family table are technology-free zones. Set the example with your own electronic devices. He will grow up in the habit of conversing with you at mealtimes; then later in the afternoon, and after doing his homework he can chat with his friends on social networks for periods no longer than 20 minutes. The length of time you allow him for this will depend on his having done his homework.

Less time on the computer and cell phone and more conversation, board games, walks and sports with the family. While still a young child, let him get used to having a human relationship with those he loves and with those who love him, above and beyond any of his personal activities. Let him get used to having pleasurable experiences with you and the rest of the family and not to being attached to an electronic device. Let him learn that these devices are useful for work and study but not for creating closer family ties and friendships.

Teach him that his room has an open door through which Mom or Dad may enter whenever they need to. This open door policy regarding his bedroom should be established from the very start. Even though modern psychology recommends respecting a child's privacy, I think it is advisable for him or her to first of all respect the limits and rules of the household. Later in life this will facilitate his or her adapting to the community of his peers and to the limitations that society says we must not transgress. Not only should the home be a haven of moderation and love but also a place where one learns of the demands of life. Let him know: Mom and Dad worked hard to buy this house. Tell him, When you grow up and have a job, you'll be able to buy your own place and make your own rules. Keep in mind the importance of preparing him for the real world even if your own economic status is idyllic.

The importance of playing with your child

Playing with your child is an early kind of *conversation*. If he smiles and engages with you, he will confide in you in the future. I mean playing with him daily. This will free up the little girl inside you. Play without being in a hurry. Roll around with your child on the carpet. Build a Lego house, paint, draw, make stick figures with him. Don't be watching the clock to end it quickly. This activity is beneficial for both of you. It helps to create an emotional relationship and interaction. There is no need for complicated or expensive toys. Let him look for anything within reach and transform it into a beautiful house or castle.

When I go to my granddaughter's home, we pretend we are making a fort, just as she does with her mother, my daughter. We make use of two large umbrellas, some living room chairs and blankets and, with them, we built a fort. Then we slip inside, chatting half in English, half in Spanish. We fashion clay figures and tell each other funny stories. If suddenly, in her fantasy it starts to rain, this gives us a great excuse to hug each other and to share a steaming cup of tea with imaginary cups and saucers.

Try it today. It is a special and enriching experience which is beneficial for your emotional state. You will forget about your problems at work and your stress will go away. You will clear your mind while at the same time create a sacred connection with your child that nothing can destroy. I recommend this as a daily exercise. I know what you're thinking; "Do I have time for this…?" Well, try to make the time and you will see changes in your character and in your child. Remember, *the length of time you are with your child is just as important as the quality.*

What your child must learn at this stage

From birth to age six, your child needs to acquire skills of enormous significance in order to assure his personal development into adulthood. Guided by the hand of Mom and Dad he will have learned the meaning of order in the human family. He will become an autonomous and authentic human being. He will have developed certain essential skills and values for living in society—conditions for the human spirit without which we will come to an end as a species. These conditions are as follows:

> *The capacity to feel guilt.*
> *The capacity to be alone.*
> *The capacity to acquire ethical and moral values.*
> *The capacity to express kindness and compassion.*

The capacity to feel guilt

You must create for your child an emotional and physical setting to allow him or her to develop the capacity to acknowledge guilt or what we call a feeling of guilt. Your child will not develop a personality suited for life in society unless he or she has properly developed this capacity. That is, your child must have an optimal family environment in which he or she develops a healthy concern for others rather than indifference, and shows compassion rather than cruelty. Earlier in this book, I stated that genetic and congenital inheritances are unknowns. WE DO NOT KNOW the nature of the genetic material our child comes into this world with nor do we understand the experiences of intrauterine life. Therefore, his or her inclinations and predispositions will remain hidden until they are either brought out or suppressed by the family atmosphere. *To be a good father or good mother means to ensure the development of your child's positive inclinations and to suppress the negative ones.*

During the first few months of his life, as we noted, an infant experiences intense moments of anxiety, especially the frustrations caused by hunger, sleeplessness, etc.—stimuli that he registers, as was explained, with his *receptive* system. Even though he doesn't relate to you as a person, he does relate to the breast that nourishes him. According to psychoanalyst Melanie Klein the infant perceives your breast either as a "bad breast" if it frustrates him and doesn't feed him properly, or as a "good breast" if it feeds him with love. These experiences give rise to the love/hate impulses that will finally merge when he recognizes you as his mother—the possessor of that breast as someone other than himself. Loving and hating the same person is a well-known ambiguity in human beings. This ambiguity reveals itself in two contrasting tendencies manifested in a child's behavior. For example, he may kiss his mother, and then proceed to bite her without warning. Providing a "good breast" is a precondition for the normal development of every human being. It is a protection against the hate impulse he feels toward you when you leave him and allows for the repairing of this hate impulse and its consequences by creating in him a feeling of guilt.

There are some people who never feel guilt or remorse and who lack any concern for others. Such people are called antisocial or psychopathic because they have not had an enabling environment to help them develop feelings of concern for others. They've grown up with the type of mother, and perhaps a family, lacking in feelings of empathy or the capacity to imagine themselves in someone else's shoes. Given that we are bio-psycho-social beings, such a mother can be the trigger for negative genetic predispositions in a youth who, if he also has a psychopathic brain, could become a murderer or an unscrupulous person. Let me share an example. Neurobiologist and professor emeritus at the University of California, Dr. James Fallon discovered, when he saw a scan obtained from his own brain showing the same anatomical conformation typical of that of a psychopath—anomalies related to the areas of self-control, empathy and emotion. As you can imagine, he was totally astonished. This experience inspired him to write a book entitled Inside a *Psychopath's Brain* in which he speculated about the reasons why, in spite of the anatomical conformation of his brain, he had become a renowned and respected scientist, a friendly and approachable person. He found his answer in the fact that he had had loving, reliable and affectionate parents—parents who were able to prevent the activation of his psychopathic tendencies. This is holistic. A disease, in order to manifest itself, must have an environmental trigger to prompt the inclinations of our DNA and the characteristics of our brain. We must be careful!

The capacity to be alone

Solitude is learned in the company of Mom. By being by your side, your child will be taught this important capacity. You instill confidence in him. You dispel his fears. You are there, inside him. Your breast is reliable and good. This capacity to be alone depends on a good mother being there in one's psyche, in one's soul and heart. Over time, a child will feel safe and satisfied even in the absence of good situations or good people. The mother or the "good breast," integrated in the child's mind will always depend on there having existed for the child an environment in which instinctual gratifications were frequent and satisfying—an environment that provided nourishment, adequate shelter and love; an environment where there was also a sufficient dosage of frustration—just enough. This will create a safe internal environment—that of a protective mother who is tucked into his heart (internalized). How to make this happen? Ponder this: the child's *self* is like a plant that needs to be cared for. He needs his mother, as stated earlier, as his "assistant self"—an *orthopedic self*. He will also need this in order to acquire the experience of solitude. When he is by himself, without you, if he is emotionally weak he will have feelings of helplessness. But if he has you in his heart and soul, this will not happen. The capacity to be alone lies at the very root of security and basic self-esteem. I am not referring to being alone in an empty room, but rather the ability to enjoy solitude, be alone, not needing people, objects or circumstances to confirm one's happiness. The mother, now internalized in the child's mind, assures for him a life without needing a walking stick. In the life of an adult, situations can occur that undermine circumstantial self-esteem, such as receiving a bad grade in college or being rejected by a loved one. These situations, however, cannot harm our basic self-esteem or personal well-being attained in the earliest years of our life.

The capacity to acquire ethical and moral values
In a world where, as stated by Oscar Wilde, we know the price of everything and the value of nothing and in

which money has become what we most value, you must teach your children ethical and moral values—right from wrong. First, *educate him*; then *instruct him*. The school and the university provide him with instruction. A moral education is what you must give him. An instructed man can become a scholar but he can never be a wise man if he has no regard for others. Values are like highways and a compass to guide us. Remember, *"Freedom is learned within the context of limits"*. To be free means to know the limits that separate me from my fellow creatures, while at the same time acknowledging my connection to them.

Instill in your children the exercise of morality and ethics—two words that are often used interchangeably but have different meanings. The word *moral*, from the Latin word *mos* means custom—a set of shared and accepted norms that allow us to live together in an orderly and peaceful way in society with respect and appreciation for the needs of others; that is, the next person, one's equal , one's fellow man.

In addition to morality, inculcate ethics in your child—a term derived from the Greek *ethos*, which originally referred to the habitats of animal species, the meaning of which was later modified to refer to the consciousness or inner dwelling of humans. It is that silent but implacable voice that whispers to us at night while resting our heads on a pillow that rewards or punishes our daily actions.

Four core values are the basis for teaching the remaining well-known values: *freedom, responsibility, fairness and truthfulness.* The first instils in us the concept of freedom to determine our own fate beyond the wishes of parents and without undermining the fate of my neighbor. My limits, your limits. These two intersect. They stimulate each other without clashing. This allows us to discover the value of responsibility, to live up to commitments and to conduct ourselves in the proper exercise of our freedoms. In this way, we treat everyone with fairness and deal equitably with anyone and everyone who crosses our path. By such conduct, we show that we value truth. Aristotle said that truth is the only democratic thing in existence because everyone claims to possess a part of it. If you as a mother make use of your freedoms responsibly and fairly within the family, your son or daughter will come to understand that while there may not be just one truth, one can find a truth that is conducive to living harmoniously together.

How can one teach values in the home? This can be done through exemplary conversations. You will lose authority over your child if you talk to him about freedom and at the same time prevent him from pursuing his calling because it runs contrary to what you wish for him.

Follow through on what you say. If you promise to play ball with him or reward his good grades, don't fail to do it or you'll be teaching him to be irresponsible.

You must try hard not to lie if you don't want him to lie. Be fair in your dealings so he will practice fairness. Don't substitute your maternal or paternal relationship for money. He should love and appreciate you for your affectionate generosity and not for your credit card. I'm Sorry. I know it's easier to fork out money than to give of your time. But if this applies to you, you should consider changing the way you think. Remember, your lessons are beams of light that illuminate the pathway of his early years. Give guidance, examples and let them be clear and honest. Be there for your children. Be the North Star, the compass and the beacon that always shows the way during the darkest moments of their lives.

Ortega y Gasset said that even the most beautiful of paintings must have a frame in which to be displayed. The frame may not be worth much but without it the painting can't be displayed. Frameworks, limits. Limits and wings. Awareness. Wings on which to soar. Limits to be respected.

The capacity to express kindness and compassion

It seems that in today's world to be kind is no more than a relic of the past. Everybody is doing his or her own thing and doing nothing together. There is no listening, no mutual understanding. "Where words are not sovereign, Babel reigns" asserts Argentine thinker Santiago Kovadoff. Let us remember that the city of Babel was never built because people looked upon outsiders as aliens and not as fellow human beings.

Dr. Montessori stated that good manners are the lubricant of social relationships. *Please, May I, Thank you*—etiquette that acknowledges others in their human dimension, as existing, next to me. How often do we enter an elevator and other faces ignore us. People push and shove, alienated inside their bubbles. Teach your child to be sincere and friendly, to say *Hello* and ask permission, to say *Thank you*—magic words that prompt smiles and promote good human contact.

What kind of society do we want to create? What chip will you implant in your child's mind? What kind of example will you be? Don't complain later on.

CAPÍTULO VI

INTERACTING WITH YOUR TEENAGER

First of all, we should try to understand what it is to be a teenager. The Latin-based word *adolescence*, i.e. the teenage years, connotes suffering or hurt, a time of crises. The question is: what is the nature of this suffering and these crises? To separate the wheat from the chaff, it should be noted that an individual's childhood and infancy will be a determining factor in the kind of life crises and the degree of suffering he or she will go through during adolescence.

We can affirm, in principle, that adolescence is a social creation, a cultural construct. Through the research of anthropologist Margaret Mead, we know that certain tribes condense this period in a ceremony in which children, from one day to the next, are considered adults. Hence it is incorrect to affirm that the crises young people go through at this stage are a consequence of their being adolescents. Quite the contrary, the life crises of every young person are what define his or her adolescence. And their life crises will be determined by what they experience between birth and the beginning of their adolescence.

So, adolescence isn't something that happens by decree. Moreover, youth who work and study, in some cases do so while bearing the burden of caring for siblings and/or parents. And for those who live and work in rural environments, adolescence does not transpire with the same intensity of that of city teens. Even in large cities we can find productive teenagers with few serious problems.

It is erroneous to place adolescence into a rigid timetable and in stereotypes applicable to all teenagers. The first and foremost error is to think of all teenagers as being the same. Each individual experience has its own characteristics and, once again, it will depend on the circumstances of their childhood years.

To consider all teenagers as identical and to predict that since he/she is a teenager he/she will go through this or that pre-established crisis, is to assume that life's happenings are just a series of specific stimuli, like knee reflexes. The doctor bumps your knee and you involuntarily lift your leg—it's the same for everybody. On the contrary, depending on what happens to each one of us, our reactions will be different, based on the our resources to cope with change, our degree of self-esteem and the degree of our family's moral support. There are many things to take into consideration.

Under the social label *adolescence*, three stages have been described: early, middle and late. According to psychological studies, this phase lasts from age 12 to 28. You may wonder how this length of time has been determined. Perhaps it seems too long, especially in the United States where youth start living alone at age 17. In psychology there is a saying that when a son or daughter reaches age 20 or more parents will then be able to see the results of how they have brought them up. While respecting this average, I must point out that there are significant physiological changes in puberty that produce complex anatomical and cerebral transformations, many of which you may be familiar with, especially because of the abundant science-based commentaries available on the Internet and in the televised media. However, there are some ignored aspects that I wish to address. For example, the white brain matter responsible for the intercommunication of neurons develops very slowly, beginning at birth, progressing from the back of the brain to the frontal lobe. This frontal lobe or prefrontal cortex is the part of the brain where planning, reasoning and the controlling of impulses takes place. This part of the brain is not suffused with white matter until around age 22; some experts say as late as the 28th year. This implies that a youth, before reaching age 20, finds himself in the *limbo* of adolescence, perhaps without adequate encouragement from the family, such as having parents who won't listen to him, who spends much time alone in his room with his video games. Such a youth is very likely to make inappropriate decisions, to lose his way. However, a teen who has always had caring and attentive parents will be able to compensate for the absence of this white matter by absorbing "parental matter" during his brief formative years.

The fear of saying *No*

Parents are afraid to say *No*, lest their children be traumatized. We just let him have his wish, so he can express himself, so he can be free, so he can be creative. With this approach we will only succeed in making of our son or daughter an inconsiderate person, a slave to and ruled by his/her whims. "No" should be used profusely. You should "inebriate" your teenager with limits set with love. You are not in your children's lives to gratify them or to please them, to be their friend. You're there to educate them.

You're not his friend, you're his parent

Many parents become "buddies" to their children. They believe that by being this way, their kids will tell them everything, that they will be their friends. In the meantime, parents feel that, for them, time has not passed. They wear fashionable jeans and go out with their kids as equals. Don't fool yourself. You're not their equal. There must be an obvious inequality—a vertical structure in which the "NO" you impose on him/her is an authoritative command no matter what their desires are, or if they have an "I'll do as I please" attitude. When they are adults, and when they can stand on an equal footing with you, then you can be their friend.

Make it clear to your children from earliest childhood, that there are rules to be obeyed in the home, such as taking a bath at a scheduled time, cleaning their rooms and arranging their books, asking for things politely, never screaming. Of course, if you yourself scream or get angry, your kids will imitate you. They "photocopy" their parents' behavior.

Let them know that their bedroom is a place Mom and Dad have provided for them but does not belong to them and that you (the parents) can go in there and check on their things whenever you need to. Assure them that when they grow up and have jobs they can buy their own home and lock their doors. Then they will be able to make their own life decisions. In today's world many teenagers have the habit of locking their bedroom doors when they go out. Talk to your sons and daughters about returning home at established times and instill in them the need to ask permission. I always told my own children that life offers neither prizes nor punishments, but only *consequences*. You are not their friend. I am unwavering on this point. You are their parent. What I'm going to tell you next is especially important. Pay attention: *If you don't establish lim-*

its for your children, with love, society will impose them harshly. Teens who commit crimes were once children being raised without restrictions. For every situation there must be boundaries. Consider this: On highways, roads and runways there are lines, dots, or lights that show the way. Without them we would wander in the dark, blindly, aimlessly. Provide for your children a brilliantly lit pathway so that their lives will be peaceful and wholesome.

Talking about sex

The subject of sexual relations is quite complicated, but we will try to simplify it. Many parents, fearing that their son or daughter might be involved in sexual activity outside the home, allow them bring their "lovebirds" home to spend the night. This is not the best thing. Every parent must make his/her own decisions in this matter. I agree that sons and daughters can spend most of their free time at home with their friends, girlfriends or boyfriends, socializing. Be supportive. It's always better for them to enjoy themselves at home, even if it means more work for us parents. Of course, once again, we have to draw the line. The girlfriend or boyfriend in question can spend the day at our place, but at night he/she should definitely go home.

Talk to them indirectly about sex. If they ask to bring up the topic, all the better. If not, there are many other ways to do this, such as watching a documentary together or talking about things that are going on in the world. On the subject of sex it is not a good idea to *prohibit*; it is better to guide. Of course to be able to guide our sons and daughters, the custom of talking things over with them from an early age, should be established.

Your teenager's first love affair

Showing respect for your teenagers' boyfriends or girlfriends and to welcome them into the family circle is critical to the health of the parent-child relationship. In particular, I appeal to mothers for whom the son's girlfriends never seem to be quite good enough. I speak from authority in this matter because I am the mother of a man who was once a teenager. In this, of course I include fathers with regard to their daughters.

The boyfriends and girlfriends of your sons or daughters must be treated warmly. Prejudice has no place. When they bring a friend home, it is on their own initiative because they want to share that person with you. Somehow and with pride they introduce you to a person they have chosen and are happy with, someone toward whom they feel something akin to love.

What should our attitude be in such cases? Always direct questions and comments first to the boyfriend or girlfriend. Be sweet. Ask him/her what he/she would like to eat. Start a conversation. Avoid awkward comments. Establish rules gently but firmly. Show him/her that he/she can trust you, that you care about him/

her without using any labels, not "the girlfriend" or "the boyfriend," but someone you sincerely want to get to know.

Remember; first speak to him or her, then to your son or daughter. This approach will reinforce the filial relationship and will create an enabling environment for creating tolerance and patience. Make your home an open-door home where *discrimination has no place.*

Unimagined ways of leading your child into addiction

When we talked about perpetuating a child's permanence at home, we touched on a very delicate subject— that of a child who is used by the mother as a kind of "drug" to calm her anxieties, perhaps enduring an unhappy marriage, an unresolved trauma in her life. Often, such a woman is living with a man who puts up with her children as long as they don't bother him. He shows no interest in laying down the law of the father. Situations of this kind are very dangerous because not only do we hinder or children from achieving their independence but we can also lead them into addiction, into solving their problems by turning to substances, objects, situations or bad influences. Drug abuse can best be combatted with dialogue because addiction is basically a communication disorder. When a youth is faced with a problem with his/her significant other or has an unresolved emotional trauma, a psychologist may be able to help. Talk these things over in the family. The word "addict" comes from the Latin *a-dictio* which means "without words". That is, in the absence of an explanation for what is happening to a person—a verbalization of a conflict—these kinds of pathological destructive addictive behaviors can occur, by turning to a momentary calming substitute to create a false sense of well-being. I know that it is very difficult to face these situations. That is why there is an urgent need to create the *University of the Family*—an institution that can address and work on resolving all these issues. It is a matter of finding a balance between the two extremes of bonding and distancing. A widely dispersed family will disintegrate whereas an overly-bonded one will tend to hinder the growth and differentiation of its members. In both cases, it is always the children who are the losers. Let us search for a middle ground and create a holistic solution.

Think about it. If you don't want your son or daughter to become addicted to drugs, don't let him or her become your "drug of choice." Don't rely on or abuse over-the-counter substances. Don't keep a medicine chest full of medications and take an aspirin, or something, else for whatever is bothering you. Don't consume alcohol or smoke as a way to ease the tensions of the day. Take note, you will not be able to establish authority in the matter of drug abuse if, in front of your child, you ingest something, no matter how harmless you think it is. Nor will you have any authority on the subject of indulgence if you are also into compulsive shopping. This is known as non-substance addiction, but addiction nevertheless.

In the United States it is common for women under the extreme demands of children, work, family and going to the gym, to resort to using *Ritalin* or other such drugs to give themselves an extra boost to enable them to cope with everything they are trying to do. *The best energy supplement and the best boost is to have a healthy emotional life—a good marital relationship and a good relationship with one's children.*

Rites that heal

Family meals without electronic devices
Listen to your children when they want to talk
Never mistreat them in any way

Family meals without electronic devices
From the very beginning, teach your children that meals are a family affair, that this has already been decided. Set the table nicely. Assign everyone his/her place. Share and converse with your husband and children as all of you share a meal together. This family ritual is important, as you know, but, unfortunately it has mostly been forgotten. Consider this: When sharing a mean and your child puts food in his mouth he is not only taking

in the nourishment necessary for his physical health but he is also taking in your images—the image of Mom and Dad. It will enter into his heart and soul where it will become a shield against life's onslaughts and dangers. It will be food for his spiritual health. When your child reaches adolescence undoubtedly he or she will goof up or stumble. He or she will definitely get into mischief, get into trouble. We all have. However, he/she will not go terribly wrong, will not self-destruct. He/she will know how to evade threats to his/her integrity.

Don't bring cell phones or other electronics to the family table. Turn off the TV. Mealtime is a time of *communion and communication*. By observing these rules, you'll be telling your child that he/she is important, that your ears are totally open to listening to his/her points of view which deserve to be heard, even the simple things. Almost all the problems that adolescents are faced with are due to chronic disorders in the way families communicate. And by engaging in certain behaviors, such as getting too many tattoos, cutting oneself (a common disorder among adolescents), acquiring bad friendships, smoking or running away from home, your son or daughter is communicating his/her need for parental guidance. Of course as parents we find it more comfortable to believe that our son or daughter was just born like that, so we say, "It's not my fault" or "He went wrong." I'm sorry to burst your bubble, folks. As the saying goes, "*Wake up and smell the coffee!*" My dear colleagues, father-mother, this is not the case. Barring psychological disorders, we can state that a problem child is one who learned bad behavior at home, within the family. Of course we know that everyone is born with certain inclinations and tendencies. It is also true that everyone's brain chemistry is different. There are unknowns and this is why we need to be watchful of our attitudes towards our children. It is possible for us as parents to unknowingly trigger a negative genetic predisposition or even to prevent its development.

What will happen if you don't take the time to provide for the rites mentioned earlier? Let's say you work all day and it's really not possible to have dinner or lunch with the family on a regular basis. In such case, you can always borrow some time from your nap or rest period. It's something you should think about custom designing. Let's say you come home from work and your youngster has already had his supper and is in his room. Attention! Why not prepare a glass of orange juice or a cup of tea and share them with him/her face-to-face? Ask him/her how his/her day went. If he/she doesn't want to say anything, don't insist. Instead, tell him/her how your own day went and he/she will gradually open up to you. Put off your need to relax in front of the TV. Your stress will get even worse if you watch the news. Believe me, there is no better way to find relaxation than to immerse yourself in the world of your son or daughter. Take delight in them. Another possibility is to schedule at least one day a week to have dinner, lunch or breakfast together with the family. You can pick the day. These attentive actions on the part of the parents are to the children what a foundation is to a building. Remember a child needs his parents just as he needs calcium, proteins or amino acids. *As parents we provide nourishment for his psychological organism.* We must take care not to raise a child in a state of *emotional anorexia.*

Listen to your son or daughter when he/she wants to talk
How often has your son/daughter told you, "I need to talk to you," and you, in a big hurry, tell him/her, "I can't right now; we'll talk later." Later never arrives or, if it does, it can absolutely be too late. He needs you now; he wants to confide something important—something that has happened in his life with a friend or at school, perhaps involving a teacher. Many sexually abused children and adolescents do not have the necessary confidence of their parents—that intimacy that provides a barrier against sadness, discouragement and low self-esteem. Put your trust in them. Whatever he tells you will be held sacred. Later there will be time to verify the veracity of what he has told you.

Never mistreat your child in any way
I know it's difficult and frustrating to find out that your child has done something irresponsible, like failing to

study for a test or getting into a fight with a classmate. It's always the same. You think, "Here I am, struggling to make a living, and all this slacker does is give me problems." Ponder a while. Take it easy. You will gain nothing by insulting, punishing or denigrating him. If you follow such a course of action, over time he will become addicted to conflict. Repetitious arguments and confrontations lead nowhere. Stop! You must know that a child who is systematically subjected to this kind of abuse will lack compassion and could become a cruel person. The area of the brain that controls emotions, called the amygdala, is 12% smaller in children who have been subjected to verbal, physical or emotional abuse. If your child's natural inclination is to be indifferent or if he displays psychopathic traits, you can trigger these behaviors.

Take advantage of your teenager's defiant or questioning attitude toward rules and regulations and open up a dialogue in which you hear him out. Never reject what your son or daughter says, no matter how illogical it may sound. Open up the conversation with helpful expressions like: "What you say may be quite true, but may I give you my point of view…?" In your conversations, mention the names of certain authors or the titles of books you may have read. If you yell at him saying, "What the heck do you know!" this will not help. To belittle him is not the right approach. Neither is it the right approach to make yourself look like you know everything. Do just the opposite, and extol your son's or daughter's positive qualities. No one can grow if they are standing in someone's shadow. Just as flowers wither under the shadow of a leafy tree, your child will wither if he's standing in your shadow. For him, your achievements feel unattainable.

Neither should you compare him to his brother or sister who always does everything right. If you do this, you will create another shadow whose darkness will cause him to wither. Or perhaps—and herein lies a real danger—he will try to prove to you that he can do even better through involvement in illicit activities. Watch out! The teenage "black sheep" of the family will find friends and strangers outside the home who will benefit from and take advantage of his insecurities, and could make his situation even worse.

It is not a good idea to refer to the accomplishments of your own youth by comparing them to his academic performance. Such an attitude usually has a negative effect when a son or daughter does not perform according to parental expectations. By doing so, you will only worsen the situation. This is especially true if you are, in fact, someone at the top of your profession. If this is the case, admit to him that you're not perfect, that everything you have achieved has been by defeating hopelessness, fear and obstacles. Tell him that in life one often fails and that, through perseverance, success can be achieved in the end. In short, he needs to know that you were once in a situation similar to his.

Your teenager is endowed with great creative capability. He is curious and full of original ideas. Take advantage of this situation and open up to him with a sense of humor and bring this out in him. Under such conditions, hormones are activated that stimulate the immune system and help bring the family together through such enjoyable and pleasurable conversations.

In short, sons and daughters need to learn and follow clearly laid down guidelines conveyed assertively in a quiet voice with eye contact. Tolerance and patience are the key. Parents who scream at their children, in most cases, give in later. Before meting out punishment, make sure to follow through. Children do not need parents with inflated egos. They need human beings with whom they can share experiences, commune and communicate through the sacred chalice of family togetherness.

EPILOGUE

Motherhood, a source of true feminine power and societal repair, provides the nutrients necessary for our existence. We women hold in our hands the key to rising above the deplorable present state of affairs and to acquiring faith in and belief in the family—mankind's most important institution since his appearance on planet Earth. Within the family we discover the great philosophies of life—values that enable us to survive and to live in harmony, values that provide a framework. Like a religion, they link us to something greater than ourselves: rules, horizons and limits—coordinates for our existence that make our existence possible because of others, for others, and with others. This framework reminds us of our precarious human condition which requires limits, patience, understanding and responsible love. Dear female friend, I would ask that you help me to disseminate widely this message of solidarity and commitment, especially to our daughters and granddaughters, to our female friends and future mothers and to your significant other. I would ask that you help me to spread the message of these pages to illuminate the pathway on a journey for the healing of our children and ourselves. May it become a reality in the form of a core curriculum for the University of the Family. You, dear friend and mother, are a life-giver, the captain of a ship which without you, will never reach the promised shores of peace and hope for all.

BIBLIOGRAPHY

Bollas, Christoffer. *La Sombra del objeto*. Amorrortu *Editores*. Buenos Aires, page 35.

Winnicott, Donald. *Primitive Emotional Development*, 1945, International Journal of Psycho-Analysis, *Transitional Objects and Transitional Phenomena* 1951, International Journal of Psycho-Analysis . *Los procesos de maduración y el ambiente facilitador. Estudios para una teoría del desarrollo emocional, Editorial* Paidós, Buenos Aires, 1996, p. 193.

Castoriadis, Aulagnier, Piera. *La violencia de la interpretación.* 1992 Amorrotu Editores. Buenos Aires

Spitz, Rene. *El primer año de vida del niño*, Buenos Aires, *Ediciones Fondo de cultura económica*, 1966. *Primary Maternal Preoccupation*, 1956.

Mahler, Margaret. *The Psychological Birth of the Human Infant. Symbiosis and individuation*, 2012, Karnak Ediciones.

Tustin, Frances, *Estados autísticos en los niños*. Chapter I. *Autismo primario normal y autismo patológico*. Editorial Paidós-Buenos Aires 1994.

Klein, Melanie. Volume I. *Amor, culpa y reparación.* Editorial Paidós Ibérica, 1990.

Freud, Sigmund. *Proyecto de Psicología para neurólogos. La vivencia de satisfacción,* 1895 *Obras completas* (*Psychology for Neurologists project. The experience of satisfaction, 1895. Complete Works. Amorrotu editores, 1978.*)

N. Ferro. *El instinto maternal o la necesidad de un mito.* Madrid, Ediciones Siglo XXI, 1991.

Mintegui, C. Diez. *Maternidad, ¿Hecho natural?* Barcelona, Ariel, pp 155-185.

Levi-Strauss, C. *Las estructuras elementales del parentesco.* Editorial Paidós, Barcelona, 1981.

Bruce Fink. *A Clinical Introduction to Lacanian Psychoanalysis. Theory and Technique.* Harvard University Press, 1956..

PHOTOGRAPHY:
Chaviano studio & production Corp.

ILLUSTRATIONS

www.ingramcontent.com/pod-product-compliance
Lightning Source LLC
Chambersburg PA
CBHW070427290526
45791CB00005B/1876